Drone Start-UP 101
Finding Your Fortune in The Drone Industry

By Allen and Andrea Beach

Make No Mistake About it, Drones are the 21st Century Gold Rush!

Our mission is to help you find success the way you define it. We want to do no less than help you find your passion. Find your passion and you will find your wealth. Join us in the adventure!

Join us as an entrepreneur and enjoy a life of inspiration, challenge, and countless rewards!

Drone Start-Up 101
A *Be A Wolf* Company

www.beawolf.com

This book is dedicated to our
Children and Grandchildren.

May they have the good fortune
to find and pursue their passion in life.

Acknowledgements

Drone Start-Up 101 is our second book in a planned series of entrepreneurial books. Our first book <u>Be A Wolf ~ The Entrepreneur's Guide to Becoming a Leader of the Pack</u> was published in 2009. Both books are now available on Amazon and are focused on helping you succeed as an entrepreneur. Writing a book about our experiences has been an adventure of its own. We could not have accomplished this without those who have dedicated their time and energy to the success of both our companies. We would also like to add a Special Thanks to the "Trail Blazers" below for taking the time to share their Drone Start-Up Stories (Chapter 8):

<u>**Trail Blazers:**</u>

<u>**Richard Gill.**</u> Richard is the President and Founder of Drone Defence providing Anti-Drone Systems and Services www.dronedefence.co.uk

<u>**Debin Ray.**</u> Debin is the Co-Founder and Managing Director of Desert Rotor, providing Ground Control Systems for Unmanned Vehicles www.desertrotor.com

<u>**Bob Schmidt.**</u> Bob is the President and Founder of UAV Propulsion Tech providing UAV Technology from around the Globe www.uavpropulsiontech.com

Note – *You will find some foundational overlap between our first Book "Be A Wolf" and our second book "Drone Start-Up 101". Be A Wolf has business start-up lessons that can be applied to any business, as such and as appropriate. Some of those lessons are repeated in Drone Start-Up 101.*

TABLE OF CONTENTS

Drone Start-Up 101

Introduction

About the Authors

DRONE START-UP 101
Introduction

If you've picked up this book you probably already have at least a streak of the entrepreneurial spirit within you. It's that inner yearning to strike out on your own and seek your own fortune. That urge to leave behind familiar (and maybe even tiresome) territory to blaze a new trail. It's an itch to rise out of the rank and file and become a successful entrepreneur. It's the belief that there has to be something more than the status quo "hire and retire" kind of life, the thirty-year grind until you gain the reward of your pension plan—if it still exists—and *finally* enjoy the good life. Whether your desire is to run a small Drone company out of your garage or to be the head of a multimillion-dollar Drone corporation, join us on an amazing journey that will challenge and reward you in ways you could never have imagined.

More than twenty years ago we turned our backs on secure, successful careers in corporate America to become entrepreneurs and we've never looked back. On the surface, we had it all: management positions with top-tier companies, financial success, the respect of our superiors and colleagues. All signs indicated that we'd continue a steady ascent up the corporate ladder and eventually ease into a cushy and well-deserved retirement.

In short, we had made it. But despite all this, we still found ourselves with a restlessness that could only be assuaged in one way. Some people fantasize about building a dream home or going on a dream vacation. We fantasized about launching a dream company, and we made that dream a reality. We got the fairy-tale ending! In fact: not only have we had the privilege of creating exactly the kind of company we'd always wanted, pursuing a career we loved, and fulfilling a long-cherished dream to be in business for ourselves, we made millions of dollars doing it. Add to this that we were able to provide a truly remarkable work environment for employees who became like family, and life doesn't get much better. We launched our first business in 1997; Argus Connection (A Technology Services Company) that quickly grew into a Multi-Million Dollar Corporation. We sold Argus Connection in 2009, wrote a book and took several years off. The book, "Be A Wolf, The Entrepreneur's Guide to Becoming Leader of the Pack" is available on Amazon and at www.beawolf.com In 2015 we launched Argus Rising, A First Responder Drone Training Company. We completed our second book in 2017 "Drone Start-Up 101" which is available at www.Dronestartup101.com and on Amazon. We consider entrepreneurship one of life's greatest adventures offering untold rewards, both professionally and personally.

We're hardly unique in our desire to step out of the norm. During 2016 more than 500,000 new businesses were started per month in the U.S. alone. But without proper guidance, these fledgling entrepreneurs, many of them with little or no business know-how, will meet with failure.

If you don't think so, just consider how few of those nearly six million entrepreneurial dreams we mentioned met with success. Even in an environment of economic expansion, almost half of new businesses fold within the first year, and over 80% fail within the first five years. By ten years, nearly all of them are long forgotten.

Argus Rising, our First Responder Drone Training Company has not only beaten those dismal odds, it's become a greater success than we imagined. *Drone Start-Up 101* is the story of how Argus Rising was born, survived setbacks, and became successful through its formative years. It also contains a distillation of everything we know about launching and running a successful business, from the planning stages all the way up to the first million and beyond. It doesn't matter what type of Drone business you're interested in launching or growing—our story is for everyone who wants to live out their dreams and make money while doing it.

In short, *Drone Start-Up 101* is the story of how we succeeded and a guide for you to build your own successful Drone Company.

CHAPTER ONE
Drones – The 21st Century Gold Rush

When gold was found in California in the mid-1800s, it forever altered the course of America. The early miners that went to California discovered that gold was everywhere. It was literally sitting out in the open, waiting for the prospective miners to find and realize its value which is what created the greatest Gold Rush in our Nation's history. However, it was not only the miners who got rich, it was suppliers, service providers, stores, and companies, like Levi Strauss, which made a fortune selling jeans and other supplies to the miners. Today, we are in the midst of another Gold Rush created by advanced aerial technology. Drone technology is one of the very few rapidly expanding technologies that individuals can take advantage of and be a part of the on-going development process. Life as we know it is changing faster than we can imagine, creating thousands of opportunities for small innovative companies. We believe some of the most successful companies in the next 5-10 years will be Drone-based. It is like the Internet in 1992; it is poised to change the way the world works. Combine all this with the fact that Drones are the one new technology where small, nimble companies can still make serious inroads and the future is yours for the taking.

Before we get into the nuts and bolts of how to launch and run your Drone business, let us pause for a moment and tell you a little about ourselves and about how our journey took us to the gold mines of the drone industry.

As you've probably guessed already, we're a husband and wife team. We were actually business partners before we were life partners, so you could say that it was business that brought us together. (Though how to find your spouse through entrepreneurship will not be part of this book!) Like any great team we shared many things in common, and one of them was a certain restlessness that had been within us from the beginning. That restlessness turned out to be one of the strongest driving forces of our entrepreneurial spirit.

Allen grew up in a military family that picked up and moved every two years. Because of all the moves, Allen learned early on to be independent and to be comfortable with change—two extremely valuable traits for the successful entrepreneur. After high school he tried college but he had almost zero interest in sitting in a classroom. So, he left school, and by the time he was nineteen he was married and had joined the U.S. Coast Guard. He got into aviation and flew helicopter Search and Rescue missions out of Clearwater, Florida for the next four years. Clearwater was the busiest Coast Guard Air Station in the United States and his four-year tour of duty resulted in over 200 Search and Rescue missions and multiple life-saving medals.

Allen frequently says he had the time of his life flying Search and Rescue for the Coast Guard, but from the beginning, he'd known it was strictly a four-year stint. Eventually he wanted to own a company and create a different kind of lifestyle for his family than the one he'd had growing up. When the four years were up, Allen took a job in his brother's business, went back to college and earned a degree and then later earned his MBA. With a growing family to support he felt he needed more income and stability. So, he opted for the most sensible path: corporate America. He applied for a job with IBM, and when "Big Blue" offered him the position, it's hard to say who was more thrilled—Allen or his mother. "That's better than being a doctor!" she said. IBM was hugely successful, and it was the perfect corporation to settle down with, raise a family, and build a career. It offered all kinds of advancement opportunities for hard workers and eager learners, and he went right up through the ranks. By the end of his fourteen years with IBM, Allen was making an excellent salary, he was in a management position, and he was well positioned to continue rising.

So, there he was, a guy who had it all, but once again he found himself restless! The dream to own his own business was still alive and in fact growing stronger, and he knew that if he didn't make a move soon he could easily get stuck in the conventional version of life that so many people valued so highly. He also knew that to be successful in launching his own business, he needed experience outside of IBM. Sales with IBM can give you a false sense of security. When you show up with the IBM logo on your shoulder, 90% of your work is already done. He needed to know how he'd fare without the backing of an established presence like IBM. To get more experience, he accepted a position as Vice President of Sales with DecisionOne. That move turned out to be an invaluable step in gaining the experience he needed for becoming an entrepreneur.

Like Allen, Andrea was raised to believe that true success was gained by remaining with one company until you retired. Her paternal grandparents were first-generation immigrants from Czechoslovakia who came to America to pursue the proverbial

American dream, and their influence on her father translated into an "idle hands are the devil's workshop" mentality. Raised on a small Texas ranch, Andrea and her three brothers worked side by side on jobs designed to provide them with little free time and a sense of completing tasks the right way, no matter how small. Her father always stressed the importance of hard work and of getting a job with a good company and progressing through the ranks. Her first job was with Southwestern Bell, and she had every intention of remaining with them for the duration of her career.

But there was a restlessness within her, as well. She wondered, *Why not me? Why can't I forge a new path?* And as Andrea will be the first to tell you, she also had a fiercely competitive nature—not surprising, given that she was the only girl in a house with three very active brothers! Following business school and college, she eventually went to work for Sorbus, a computer maintenance company, which later became DecisionOne. For quite some time she found just what she wanted, as DecisionOne offered myriad opportunities for advancement for people who worked hard. By the early 90s she was the single mother of two incredibly wonderful children; her management position at DecisionOne provided a good life for her and her children.

All in all, DecisionOne was a positive experience, but Andrea was becoming increasingly disenchanted with the company. Because of mergers and buy-outs and the changes those developments instituted, it was becoming less and less what she wanted. By the time Allen joined the company in 1994 Andrea had been with DecisionOne for fifteen years and was a regional manager overseeing a staff of twenty, but despite the security and success, she was ready to move on. She had always dreamed of owning her own business, but as a single mom she had concerns about stepping out as an entrepreneur.

It was through DecisionOne that we met. Little did we know that we were to become partners in both business and life.

So, let us pick up the thread in late 1994. Meeting then couldn't have been better timing: we had arrived at very similar points in life, and we quickly discovered that we had a mutual passion for owning and running our own company. In 1995 we began talking about going into business together, and by the next year we were drawing up business plans and hammering out ideas of how to be successful on our own. As a *team*, however, we were brimming over with confidence and knew we could succeed.

Still, there was a lot to consider before we made the leap, a lot we could lose if our venture didn't go well. We were successful by any standard, and already halfway down the road to a long and easy retirement. There was absolutely no safety net for the plunge we wanted to take, absolutely no guarantee that the company we were on the verge of launching would ever make a dime. And that nice retirement plan, the promise of the good life for which we'd so long labored? We might as well have kissed it goodbye.

But another voice told us that there was more, much more, to life. We refused to believe that the status quo version of success that had been handed down to us from our parents' generation—that you stick with one company for thirty years and gratefully accept your pension—was the only version of the story. Don't get us wrong, we recognize that for many people

Corporate America is the right path but for us, that story left too many troubling questions unanswered. Why couldn't the good life happen *now*? Why should we spend the best years of our lives working tirelessly to fulfill someone *else's* dream? Security and stability aside, did it really make sense to remain in a vast corporate culture in which we could rarely see the impact of our efforts? And, as the voice within grew ever louder, could we live with ourselves if we didn't heed it? The answer to that last question was obvious: absolutely not!

It was time to leave behind the familiar and explore uncharted territory. We felt that come what may, we had the skills and experience to recover from any setback. So, after careful planning, we launched our first company Argus Connection, Inc. at the beginning of 1997. After selling Argus Connection in 2009 we took some time off and wrote a book about our experiences as entrepreneurs, "Be A Wolf". In 2014 we started our second company Argus Rising, a Drone Training company focused on First Responders. Pursuing a shared business dream with your life partner isn't for everyone but for us it's been a life-changing, joy-filled adventure we wouldn't trade for anything.

What an adventure it's been. Argus Connection started out in a 10' x 10' rented office in 1997 with a rented desk and chair. Our goal for the first year was sheer survival, but the business took off before we could barely register what was happening. That first year we cleared $680,000—not bad for a company of two people—and in the second year, sales were up to three and a half million. By 2001, what had begun as a technical services company had expanded to include technology staffing, and we were up to over eight million dollars in sales. While growth has been slower for Argus Rising than the original Argus, we are on track for a successful 3rd year in business and we have already received offers to purchase the company. Yes, financial freedom is wonderful, but perhaps the best thing of all is that we're doing what we love and we're doing it *our way*. We're proof positive that it's possible to create exactly the kind of company you've always dreamed of working for, to have your employees become your extended family, and to find financial success, too.

But all this, of course, is not the *end* of the story. How did we get from hearing that inner voice to actually starting the business and finally to the happy ending we're enjoying today? As anyone who's ever started a business or even contemplated doing so knows, launching a business (not to mention *staying* in business) is no quick and easy process. After years of successes and setbacks, we've got plenty of tested advice for anyone who's interested in being a successful Drone entrepreneur, and plenty of real-life stories to illustrate our points. Now that we are both officially 'seniors', one of our goals in life is to pass on to the next generation the knowledge, motivation, tenacity and resourcefulness required to build your own successful company.

There's no time like the present to get started. Let's begin with five principles that can help you in the planning stages of your business or even if you're merely contemplating stepping out on your own. In subsequent chapters, we'll take you step by step through everything from the characteristics you need to do business to finding start-up capital to marketing to long-term survival—in short, everything you need to know to launch and sustain a successful Drone business.

Business Planning Top 5 Checklist

1) Do what you know

We spent many a late night dreaming up possible business models and sketching out preliminary business plans. We did a ton of research which included learning how to fly various Drone models with different attributes. As you know, the market is thick with Drones in all shapes, sizes, costs and capabilities. As we considered starting a Drone company we were brimming over with enthusiasm and wanted to keep our options wide open, so we gave serious consideration to several different Drone business models before settling on Drone Training. (Which, via the lens of hindsight for us, seems like a no-brainer.) One of the things we considered was Drone Photography and Services. Who doesn't love the amazing photos and videos being captured by Drones? We wanted to create that experience for people and we were looking for opportunities that were dynamic and fun, so Drone Photography and Services seemed like a grand idea.

That is, for about two minutes! While this is certainly a viable business model it was not the right model for us. The truth is, we were not experienced photographers, the learning curve of both Drones and Photography was simply more than what we wanted to tackle for a startup company. It did not fit our criteria of "Do What You Know"

Fortunately, we realized that and were willing to admit it. Too many businesses have failed because people get into areas that are outside their realm of expertise. So, the first rule in launching a successful business? *Do what you know.* You must determine what will be a good fit for you. We were both very experienced in the training industry, so that's the direction we went, and it turned out to be the best possible decision.

The "do what you know" principle applies not only to determining what kind of business you launch, but once in business, what sort of role you'll play in actually running your company. Your role should be determined by what you know how to do and what you do well.

One of the things that helped us tremendously through all the years of Argus Connection and Argus Rising is that from the beginning, we've been very clear about our individual strengths. Allen is very good at sales, and Andrea is very good at building an infrastructure. We actually maintain a strict line of demarcation between these two areas of responsibility. It's not only what we want, it's a must! Allen, for instance, couldn't care less about payroll, invoices, taxes, paying rent, and so on, perhaps to an astonishing degree. Back when Argus Connection hired its very first employee, Liz, Allen still wasn't receiving a paycheck. But Liz rightly wondered when she'd be getting paid. Allen's jaw dropped. An employee paycheck? It hadn't even occurred to him! Next there was the issue of withholding taxes from Liz's earnings. Again, Allen was taken by surprise. "Let's just take a guess," he said. "It will all balance out at the end of the year." Andrea could only roll her eyes—and roll up her sleeves.

Needless to say, Allen knows a lot more about the details these days, but he still steers clear of this part of the business. We work exclusively in our realm of interests and strengths, and for us this system has paid off in spades. Our interests and strengths perfectly complement each other, which is exactly what you need in a team.

2) Figure out your worst-case scenarios and determine whether you can survive them

Neither one of us grew up with a silver spoon, so from a young age we had the advantage of knowing how to make tough situations work. We also had abundant confidence in ourselves and in each other, which made it relatively easy to turn our backs on established careers and strike out on our own.

Still, we didn't leap blindly, and we didn't proceed without extensive planning. Strange as it sounds, part of that planning was to sit down and dream up all sorts of worst-case scenarios. We examined each one and then asked ourselves, *Can we live with this?* The answer was always "Yes!" We firmly believed that no matter what happened, we could start over and recover.

We'd encourage anyone who's planning a business to do what we did and examine your worst-case scenarios. Literally write down a list of all the negative possibilities that could happen, everything from the minor annoyances to the outright disasters. Then ask yourself if you can live with each particular outcome and if possible, how you can recover from it.

If you find that you can't live with your worst-case scenario, the time may not be right to start your own business, or it may be time to find a partner who can help you through that particular situation (or better yet, prevent it). In the world of entrepreneurship, there are never any failsafe guarantees of success. Always understand the worst-case scenario—it's usually not as bad as you might think. However, a calculated leap of faith is still a leap of faith.

3) Build a corporate culture that people are excited about

We think this is such an important piece of the puzzle that we're going to devote a whole chapter to it. Here, let us merely emphasize that formulating your company culture is a task you should be engaged in from the very first minute you accept the challenge of starting your own business. Don't put it on the back burner or assume that the right culture will just naturally evolve as you proceed. Make your company culture a top priority, and let that culture permeate every aspect of how you do business.

One of the reasons we became dissatisfied with corporate America was that the big companies lost their people-focused culture of pulling together toward a common goal (if they ever had it at all). We were determined not to let that happen, no matter how large we grew. One of our first steps was to look inward; we dreamed up the kind of company culture we ourselves would love. For us, it was very important that Argus offered a culture that was different from anything we'd seen before. We wanted a company culture that would quickly and vividly establish Argus as a place that was exciting and even a fun place to work. We wanted to reward superior performance and create an environment in which employees would be family members rather than nameless faces in a huge corporate machine. We then went out of our way to create it. This was well before we'd made a dime.

We spend a lot of dollars and hours maintaining our company culture, and it's been the best investment we've ever made. Make sure your company is an exciting and fun place to work, build a feeling of camaraderie and team spirit. Do that and you'll reap the rewards of a people-focused culture. From Argus' earliest days we attracted exceptionally good talent, talent that would've otherwise been lost to other interests.

4) There is nothing more important than sales

This is an extremely important principle and we're going to devote an entire chapter to it later. But it's well worth emphasizing this principle early on because so many people make the mistake of pouring a great deal of time, money and energy into planning and building up their infrastructure before pursuing sales. We think this is absolutely backwards. It doesn't make sense to spend an inordinate amount of time planning out a company that has zero in sales—you're not a viable company until you've made a sale! Knowing this, spend your time and energy bringing in some dollars. Your sales will not only drive your infrastructure, they will drive the *correct* infrastructure. Nothing happens until you sell something.

5) *Be willing to throw out the status quo ~ "Get Creative"*

People with a creative mentality never let the conventional way of doing things restrict them or let major challenges stop them. Had we not gone against conventional wisdom, our desire to own our own business would've remained a pipe dream. We would have continued working in the great machine of corporate America, contributing to the success and profit of someone else's dream.

Sometimes the easy route will be very tempting. Before the original Argus had even been in business a month, Allen's commitment to launching the business was tested when Electronic Data Systems (EDS) called him for an interview. As he knew the EDS team well, he agreed to meet with them. EDS extended an extremely good offer—at that time, the best offer of his career. It was tempting but joining EDS would've put him right back where he had been, so he declined. The very next day, EDS came back with an even better offer and a signing bonus. There were bills to pay and no guarantee that Argus would ever get off the ground, and the EDS deal would've made life easy.

With that kind of money on the table, we decided it would be foolish not to at least consider the offer. We called an emergency powwow, during which we gave serious consideration to Allen accepting the offer, leaving Andrea to get Argus up and running. We agreed to sleep on it, but as it turned out, we didn't need that long: within hours, the phone rang at Andrea's just as she was about to call Allen.

"I just can't do it," Allen said. "I agree one thousand per cent," Andrea said. "It's time to get

Argus up and running. We can start over if we have to," Andrea said. So, we turned down an extremely lucrative offer and went out to celebrate!

Once you do make the leap and open your business, let that openness to innovation guide your business. Be willing to make changes as you find your way to success. This practice paid off wonderfully for Argus Rising which was originally a Drone Training Company for anyone that wished to use Drones commercially. When Argus Rising was still less than a year old we were contacted by a Detective with a local police force and he asked if we could develop a course specific to Law Enforcement and Fire & Rescue (First Responders). That was not our company mission but the idea of training First Responders was an exciting one. We developed a 5-day Drone "Boot Camp" for First Responders and the rest is history. Now all we do is First Responder training both Nationally and Internationally. *When opportunity knocks, even when it is outside your original idea consider it carefully, allowing client requirements to shape your company is a sure way to success.*

Some people thought we were crazy for changing direction so early in the life of the business, but our business was young and we were more than willing to try something different.

Be willing to do things no one has ever done before. It can give you a competitive edge in the market, and if you've done your homework and determined that your new way is a reasonable risk, it can pay off big.

If your dream is to own and operate your own Drone business, don't let the opportunity pass you by. Putting in your time, with little enthusiasm and operating from only a small percentage of your potential, is not good for you, nor is it good for your employer. Entrepreneurs are never willing to accept this scenario.

Act decisively. If you see a nugget lying in the stream, you owe it to yourself to pick it up. No one can guarantee that you'll meet with success. What *is* guaranteed is that there's no chance of a good ending if you don't even begin your story.

Chapter One Notes:
Drones - The 21st Century Gold Rush

- In starting your own business, do what you know. Figure out what your interests and strengths are and cater to them. You'll get nowhere fast if you leap into completely unknown territory.
- Before you even begin planning your start-up, make a list of worst-case scenarios. Ask yourself if you can recover from each of them. If the answer is yes, then go for it! If the answer is no, re-evaluate whether this is the time to go it alone, or find partners who can help you.
- Make defining and implementing an attractive company culture one of your top priorities. Create a company culture that will attract the best talent to your business. Take care of your people and they will take care of you.
- Nothing happens until you make a sale. Let your sales define your infrastructure, not the other way around.
- Never be satisfied with the status quo. Be open to changing your business model as appropriate, allowing your clients to define your business model. Some of the world's greatest accomplishments have come from innovative visionaries who were willing to change a pre-defined direction. If you do your homework, you'll be able to evaluate these opportunities as they arise.

CHAPTER TWO
It's Time to Stake Your Claim
Drone Opportunities Abound

Some of you may already be wondering if you have what it takes to be successful in the Drone industry. Well not to worry! *Drone Start-Up 101* is written with the first-time entrepreneur in mind. It's based upon the premise that anyone can evolve from an ordinary businessperson into a successful entrepreneur.

Let's begin our story in how to be a successful entrepreneur by examining potential opportunities to focus your business on, or in other words, Staking Your Claim! This discussion will help you realize the almost unlimited number of opportunities that currently exist in the Drone industry and what may or may not be a good fit for you. You cannot go a week without reading a Drone-related story, particularly new and exciting ways people have found to incorporate them into their business. It is by no means a complete list and, in fact, new opportunities for making money in the industry present themselves on an almost daily basis.

Aerial Photography

This seems to be the first thing everyone thinks of when considering a Drone based business, let's take a look at some of the possible lines of business for Aerial Drone Photography:
- Commercial Real Estate
- Residential Real Estate
- Development and Land Planning
- Construction

- Concert and Event
- Business Marketing
- Golf Course Management
- Orthomosaics
- Production Drone Photography Services
- AND the list goes on...

So, with just one opportunity "Aerial Photography" we have 9+ possible lines of business; every Drone business we can think of has numerous potential lines of business as a subset. Below we review 13 more Drone businesses. If each one averages just 10 lines of business and each line of business has 3 possible business models, that immensely multiplies the possible lines of business and that is just the tip of the iceberg. This should give you some sense of the enormity of the possible opportunities in the Drone industry.

Orthomosaics

An orthomosaic is a series of individual aerial photographs which are stitched together so that they form a single image. Land Developers, Golf Courses, City Governments, National Parks, Law Enforcement and many others need aerial surveys to fully evaluate some of their projects. In the past this has been a costly service involving helicopters and expensive cameras. Today, Drone Pilots can provide the same aerial photographs at a significantly lower cost. Drone photography also improves the quality of the final product due to auto-pilot capabilities and the Drone's ability to fly at lower altitudes capturing higher quality images.

Drones with LIDAR

We could devote an entire chapter to this technology but for the purposes of this book we will focus on the actual opportunities and not the technical details. You may also see it phrased as Lidar or LiDAR but however you see it, it stands for "Light Imaging, Detection and Ranging" and of all the individual Gold Mines that can be explored it has the potential for being one of the largest mines of all.

The Basics: In its simplest form LIDAR can measure the distance to a specific target. If you point the laser at the target, it measures the reflected pulses with a sensor. It could be a tape measure that uses a laser to measure the distance between you and say a house. Now let's make the laser a scanner so it fires a constant laser and constantly measures as it scans the topography of the target, such as a house. As it scans the house it begins to paint a 3D model of the house capturing the difference in distance between the outside wall, window frame and a door. Now merge that information with photography and it will provide a 3D photographic model of the target. This technology has actually been around for a long time, it was used by Apollo 15 to map the surface of the moon. So, why is this now a Gold Mine? The answer is twofold, the technology is far more accurate than ever before, capturing measurements to the sub-centimeter level. When you combine that with the flight capability of Drones and GPS coordinates, you create a 3D mapping technology that is in high demand for numerous industries including Agriculture, Construction, Roads, Mining, Waste Disposal, Entertainment, Geology, Surveying, Archology, Forestry, Inspections and the list goes on.

The Drone LIDAR market as of 2015 was around $16 Million; it is expected to be well in excess of $100 Million by the year 2022.

Training

As the Drone industry expands there is a real need for qualified training partners. This is the path that we chose originally, providing training to those wishing to fly commercially. Once we were presented with the opportunity to jointly develop and teach a 5-Day First Responder Bootcamp we knew this was our niche in the industry. We have since trained dozens of Law Enforcement, Firefighters and First Responders. Argus classes now include:

- Top Gun 5-Day Boot Camp
- Top Gun 3-Day Crime / Accident Scene Orthomosaics
- Top Gun 2-Day Search and Rescue (SAR)
- Top Gun 2-Day Active Crime / Fire Surveillance (ACS)
- Top Gun 2-Day Active Shooter
- Top Gun 2-Day Tether Deployment (TD)
- Top Gun 2-Day Thermal Imaging (TI)
- Top Gun 2-Day Chemical Spill, Hazardous Site Inspection

These are our chosen lines of business but in fact you could pick just one of these and potentially run a business; i.e., offer a 3-Day Search and Rescue [SAR] Camp that provides training for First Responders to learn advanced SAR techniques.

Aerial Inspections

Inspections is a broad category with so many possible lines of business that we have elected to simply pick one "Power Utility Inspections" and explore the related business models. It is feasible that in the near future every power utility truck will carry a Drone and every Lineman will be required to possess an FAA pilot license in order to quickly conduct power line inspections. Possible business models are:

- Drone Training specific to Lineman and their respective jobs
- Drone Inspection Services provided by a team that can respond to Power Utility Inspection requests
- Value Added Reseller (VAR) services tailored to sell Drones specifically for the power utility business

Each line of business is a potential business in and of itself but they can also be combined, such as a Drone Value Added Reseller for power utilities, to also provide Training. The possibilities are nearly limitless

Marketing

Local Businesses, Golf Courses, City Governments, Real Estate Agents, and an ever-increasing number of possible clients will need aerial videos to assist them with marketing. Consider the

Drone as a tool. Where companies used to need cranes, trucks, and helicopters to get overhead shots, all you need today is a good Drone. If you already have marketing experience, adding a Drone to your tool box will provide access to additional markets and clients.

Athletics

From professional teams to minor leagues to colleges and high schools, having the ability to add an overhead view can significantly enhance the play review process for both coaches and team members. A Drone can capture great aerial videos that no one else can see from a swimmer's technique to a football play strategy to a skier on a black diamond run. These aerial videos allow an analysis of team and individual performance that coaches have never had before. If you are already a coach or involved in athletics you can demonstrate the value of aerial videos and photographs with your personal involvement.

Events

Once again there are so many possible lines of business for a Drone Event company that we could not possibly cover them all so let's take look at a popular event "Weddings" and explore the possible lines of business listed below.

- Drone Training for Wedding Photographers and their respective associates. The use of Drones allows you unlimited creative opportunities and potential and is the latest and greatest in the field of wedding and event photography

- Wedding Photographer who also provides amazing aerial photos and video. Capture the moment in a unique way
- Value Added Reseller (VAR) tailored to sell Drones specifically to Event Photographers

Each line of business is a potential business onto itself but they can also be combined, such as a Drone Value Added Reseller for Event Photographers that also provides Training.

Leasing

Leasing Drones will be a viable future business model. The ability to rent a Drone perhaps with specialized equipment will be valuable to many companies. For some it is much more cost effective to rent a Drone for a few hours or a day than to purchase one. We also suggest providing services that could range from hourly pilots to video processing. Startup can be costly as you will need to invest money in the equipment and marketing.

Video Processing

Provide video processing services specializing in the field of aerial footage. You could work with a range of clients from other Drone businesses to Law enforcement and Fire and Rescue. We received a call just the other day from a Sheriff's office looking for someone to process and provide both soft and hard copies of orthomosaics, a perfect niche business. Many Drone operators do not have video processing skills and need to outsource this service, the possibilities are limitless.

Be A Drone Resource

Become a resource company to other Drone companies. If you have web skills, or can partner with someone who does, this becomes very affordable to get started. Listed below are just a few of the possible lines of business related to Drone Resources. You can specialize with just one or combine logical lines of business into a single entity.

- Video Processing
- Web-based Pilot Resume Database
- Drone Membership Organization – such as AMA, but specifically for Drone operators and businesses (International Drone Association [IDA])
- Central Website for other Drone services
- Drone Blog / News Agency
- Drone Certifications for companies providing Drone services

Agriculture

Drones are rapidly becoming a part of today's standard agriculture tools. You can provide training specific to farmers or provide services to large and small farming operations or be a value-added reseller specifically for agriculture needs. The relatively inexpensive information provided to today's farmers allows them to spot disease and insect damage, watering issues, fencing integrity and other problems before significant damage is a reality. Today's technology reduces the cost so that smaller farmers can be more competitive with the large industrial farming units.

Litigation Support

Attorneys often require aerial photos, videos and accident scene recreation assistance. In the past this has been a very expensive and time-consuming service only available to those with deep pockets. With the advent of the Drone these services can be provided at a reasonable cost. Accident scene recreation and 3D modeling require in-depth training but these services can be very lucrative.

Aerial Surveys and Mapping

Drones utilizing Auto-Pilot have become the go-to technology for creating topographic surveys and maps. The costs of orthomosaic and 3D capture-software, along with Drone hardware, have dropped dramatically in price. This allows a detailed, unique view that's invaluable to industries like construction, land and resource management, mining, or for gathering data for any environment that needs to be monitored.

We have listed numerous possible Drone companies and multiple potential lines of business and this is not even a comprehensive list of all the possibilities! So how does one choose? Let's get back to the basics. Remember to "Do What You Know" matching your skills as best you can to your interest list. Once you have done that, look for something you can believe in, something that wakes you up in the morning ready to mine for Gold!

Passion – A Must-Have for Any Entrepreneur

"Passion" is a word that you hear so often. Ask anybody in any field—business, athletics, the arts, science—what they need to succeed, and "passion" will invariably make the list. But what exactly do they mean by this? Enthusiasm? Excitement? Strong motivation? All of the above? The answer is - all of the above and more.

There's no doubt you've got to be enthusiastic and excited about your product and your company; you must be motivated above all else to get your company off the ground and succeed. Now multiply all of that by a thousand, and you get something like what it means to have passion. Sure, we have our bad days and we've experienced our share of setbacks. But here we are years later, still waking up every morning enthusiastic about our careers and excited to work with our fellow entrepreneurs. Our motivation has never once flagged. We may be unusually enthusiastic and confident people, but we have a company and a mission that we believe in, and even on our worst days, we know we're living out our dreams. What could be better? Why *wouldn't* you be passionate about this life?

In fact, passion is so important that even if you have a mediocre (or worse!) business plan, you can still succeed. It's happened plenty of times. A good example is a friend of ours (Steve) who attended a service sales class and decided to resign his position at IBM and strike out on his own. With very little planning, he started a company selling uninterruptable power supplies (UPSs) for technology equipment. UPSs come in all sizes and prices and are designed to keep your computer running in the event that you lose power. They can cost from \$60 to over a million for a large data center. Steve's plan, such as it was, depended on two unrealistic ideas:

1. He would have to find a way to compete against IBM who had just recently started reselling UPSs to their clients.
2. He needed to get a reseller discount on UPSs that matched IBM's.

Both requirements were nearly impossible. We tried to dissuade him from resigning and instead spend some time doing more research. We pointed out that he would never be able to get IBM's reseller discount and that IBM's clients wouldn't even talk to him after he was no longer with the company. (Allen knew from experience that selling without the IBM logo on your shoulder was truly a difficult task.) There was, however, no doubt about Steve's passion. When talking to him about this new venture, you could feel his excitement and enthusiasm. He wouldn't hear of tabling the launch for any reason, or of even slowing down. He was convinced that the iron was hot and now was the time to strike. He was right about the iron being hot—his strike was just misdirected.

As predicted, Steve could not get the reseller discount that he needed, and clients with whom he'd had a personal relationship through IBM were not returning his phone calls. Three months into this venture, the news was not good. He was running on savings and had zero sales. He kept going after large deals that would create a foundation for his business but was making no progress. Still, his excitement hadn't faltered a bit, and you could hear the enthusiasm in his voice. He was basically sitting on a beach in California waiting for a sunrise. He was excited about being on the beach but all the excitement in the world wasn't going to cause the sun to rise in the West. The fuel driving him was passion and passion alone.

While passion is a necessary ingredient, passion alone will not make you successful. What it *does* do is keep you going when other people would quit. And that's exactly what happened with Steve. His passion kept him going when failure looked certain. What he really needed was to couple a new business plan with his unending passion. That's where we stepped in. We advised him to change his plan, instead of going after those large deals, he should focus on one client who would talk to him and sell that client a small UPS. Yes, we were encouraging him to start small, but the power of your first sale cannot be overstated—it's the start of everything else to come. Well, Steve did just that and four weeks later sold his first UPS for $250. He made $100 off that deal. It was four months of work and a measly hundred bucks, but you would've thought he'd hit a solid gold vein.

As always, the second sale came much easier, and then the third and the fourth came in! Soon Steve's business was up and running. Important Note – "The more business you have the more business you have access to"—*business is exponentially compounding*. Steve's slapdash business plan didn't automatically mean failure because his passion kept him going while he found his way to a plan that worked.

One day he approached a new client who had just recovered from a power outage; the client bought a UPS for every PC in the building and it was Steve's single largest sale. After that he learned to chase power outages like a personal injury lawyer chasing an ambulance—there's no better market for uninterruptable power supplies than a company that's just been burned by a power outage! He got so good at tracking power outages that he would show up before the utility repair crew. After one particular outage he spent some time talking to the repair guys and asked what had caused the outage on such a nice day. It seems a squirrel had crawled up into one of the transformers and inadvertently created a circuit between two high voltage terminals. That was it for the poor squirrel, as it was for the power supply. After that day Steve always spoke of squirrels with an unmistakable fondness. Nothing like a curious squirrel to create a week's worth of sales and a dozen new clients!

Steve now has that reseller discount he wanted and is one of the top resellers of UPSs in Texas. His passion for his business, not to mention his love for squirrels, is evident to this day.

Now let's look at the flip side. While a faulty business plan coupled with unending passion can succeed, a flawless business plan without passion will fail every time. This became evident in the dot-com bust of 2001 when so many well-funded start-ups with excellent business plans failed miserably because of a lack of real passion for the ideas. After the meteoric success and the boatloads of money so many people made, everyone wanted to get in on a good thing. Certainly, making money can provide strong motivation, but it's nothing like having an abiding passion for your company's vision and the good your product or service will bring to consumers. Thousands of people tried to get in on the dot-com bubble, believing that a good business plan and the right funding would guarantee success. We all know the end of the story. As they and so many investors discovered, this simply was not true.

A successful entrepreneur has to possess a true passion for the business. Passion brings an unwavering belief in the future and in your decisions; it is a belief that you must have to succeed. Passion will also carry you through lean times, setbacks, and even catastrophes like the financial market meltdown of 2008-09. Something we teach all aspiring entrepreneurs is the concept of "Patience and Persistence." It is your passion that will fuel your patience and persistence even when things look terribly bleak. It's passion that will get you out of bed in the morning ready to throw yourself against that impenetrable wall one more time. We've learned that when you want to give up, when everything around you screams that it's time to surrender, then throw yourself against that wall one more time and that's when it will crumble. Whether your desire is to own a Drone inspection service or franchise a Drone survey business, you have to believe in what you're doing and you have to convey that belief with a passion. If you don't have passion for your idea no else will either.

Passion multiplies; passion and enthusiasm are contagious! Your employees, your clients and everyone you come in contact with will catch the passion bug, and this passion will translate into business success.

Now for a few notes of caution.

First, whereas you have a certain amount of control over the perception people have of you, passion cannot be manufactured or feigned. You can't pretend to be passionate about something and expect everyone to believe it. True passion carries an unmistakable ring of authenticity, and people instinctively know it when they see it. You can hear true passion in a person's voice and see it in their actions.

Second, don't assume that passion, even off-the-charts passion, will bring you material wealth. The two are unrelated. Though our success in business was fueled by passion, it was a great deal of hard work that brought us wealth. Furthermore, don't confuse wealth with happiness. Our material wealth has made possible opportunities for ourselves and our family we wouldn't otherwise have, but we've done our best to teach our children never to confuse happiness in life with material things. If you believe that wealth will bring happiness, you're on a path that will end in disappointment. Don't ever forget that some of the most passionate people in the world get paid next to nothing! When Allen was in the Coast Guard in the 1970s he made $5,800 a year (That's right a Year), and to this day when he speaks of those times his passion for Search and Rescue comes through in every word.

If you want to know the connection between wealth and happiness, use whatever financial success you have to make the world a better place—*that's* where you'll find true happiness. We've been able to help a myriad of people in difficult situations that have been an outgrowth of our own personal experiences and the needs of others. While doing this doesn't generally bring you fame and fortune, it does provide a satisfaction that is sustainable. Family means everything to us—you could say that we have a passion for family—and this passion guides many of our actions. Your family can be outside the bounds of genetics and exists where you spend your time and money. Make a difference! Find your passion. If you combine passion and vision with a strong sense of your own worth and abilities, you'll be able to fuel the kind of success that engenders true and lasting happiness, whether you make a hundred bucks or a hundred million.

Chapter Two Notes:
It's Time to Stake Your Claim
Drone Opportunities Abound

- Every Drone opportunity has numerous sub opportunities that can be viewed as specialty fields and each specialty field has numerous possible lines of business as a subset making start-up drone opportunities almost endless.
- To be a successful entrepreneur, examine potential opportunities to focus your business on, or in other words, Stake Your Claim!
- Look for something you can believe in, something that wakes you up in the morning ready to mine for Gold!
- Passion brings an unwavering belief in the future and in your decisions. It is a belief that you must have to succeed.
- Combine passion and vision with a strong sense of your own worth and abilities, fueling your own brand of success. Engender true and lasting happiness that exists whether you make a hundred bucks or a hundred million.

CHAPTER THREE
Marketing On a Shoestring

Don't think of your marketing dollars as an expense but as an investment in your future. Believe it or not, it's possible to create a highly effective marketing campaign that will cost practically nothing, and we're going to tell you how. There is no master marketing model or plan that will work for every business, in other words we can't give you a specific road map to get you to your specific destination. In the end you will have to figure this out on your own for your chosen business model but what we can do is walk you through the process for developing a plan. So, let's do one together.

Stan and Kristi (Fictional Characters) live in Ohio. Stan works in Farm Tools as a salesman and Kristi is an accountant assistant. Stan and Kristi have two teenage boys that will soon be out of the house and they have frequently talked about starting their own business, the idea of having their own 'gold mine" where they reap the rewards of hard work without all the politics of corporate America is very appealing. Up to now it has only been talk, they are after all, busy raising children and making a good living. They both recognize the potential that exists in starting a Drone business as it is one of the few new technologies that lends itself well to small startups. In fact, one of Stan's clients (Jim Farmer) recently purchased a Drone to map his crops, Jim explained to Stan that the Drone allows him to see a broad overview of his fields and at the same time allows him to zoom into two inches above the plants. Jim said he can spot drought areas and bug infestation long before they become real issues, he went on to say that farmers are increasingly discovering that Drone Mapping is an invaluable tool for its cost effectiveness, ease of use and its numerous applications on the farm. He went on to say how he searched their area for an experienced Drone Pilot to do the mapping for them but he was unable to locate one. Well, that was it for Stan, when he arrived home he told Kristi "We are going into the Drone business." Let's fast forward the story, Stan and Kristi have done their homework and have decided to go into the "On-Demand Drone Pilot Service" business focused on agriculture and are now at the point that they need to develop a Marketing Plan specific to their chosen business model.

As Stan and Kristi are about to learn, marketing your Drone business is tough and can be expensive, if you are already marketing savvy or have a partner that is then you are ahead of the game. Stan and Kristi have learned that there are ways to market your Drone services or products without spending a fortune. We are going to provide several tips but you will want to spend some time developing your marketing plan specific to your business. There are also web-based Drone services that can assist you in getting started. One good example is Dronifi. They can assist you in reaching new and current clients and they can send tailored marketing collateral specific to your business, help locate new flight business and help manage your existing client base. Another is Optelos which offers workflow management and allows you to have a professionally branded portal for delivery of your photos, maps, orthomosaics, video and other data to your clients. Other online tools that may be useful are Mailchimp and Constant Contact which can assist with professional email marketing programs and the list goes on, time for doing some homework and developing a marketing strategy specific to your target market.

Stan and Kristi's chosen line of business is an "On-Demand Drone Pilot Service" which they believe will revolutionize the Drone Industry. The business model is simple, instantly connect those needing agriculture Drone services with the Certified Drone Pilots providing agriculture services. Stan and Kristi have named this company Drone Nation with a website of www.Dronenation.xxx.

Step One – Stan and Kristi need to build a brief one-page Business Model for their company like the one below, while yours will look differently you can use the same headers as a guide:

Drone Nation - Business Model:

- A user can access their site and request specific Drone Services related to Ag at a specific location and time

- Drone pilots within a pre-defined area of your request will instantly be notified of the service request and have the option to apply for or reject the request

- When Drone Pilots "Apply" the pilots photo, skill set, drone assets, pricing, rating and website, if applicable, are automatically sent to the client

- Client can then select or reject a Drone pilot from those that have applied

- Once selected the Drone pilot is notified that they have been accepted.

- Contact information will be exchanged, the client will contact the pilot and make arrangements to complete the project

- Drone Nation will hold the liability insurance covering projects and will make a copy available on-line to prospective clients

- If it is a lengthy project Drone Nation can optionally assign a Project Manager

- Important - All payment procedures are handled by Drone Nation

Drone Nation - Value Proposition:

Agriculture Clients:

- Immediate access to numerous Drone pilots and skill sets

- Has opportunity to select pilots based on skills, rating, pricing, location and assets

- Insurance accessible and held by Drone Nation

- Pay an hourly pre-set fee for the services provided

- Simplest way to complete an AG Drone project

- Ability to rate the pilot at the end of the engagement

- If lengthy, project billed weekly for approved hours

<u>Drone Pilots:</u>

- Additional source of Drone engagements

- Flexible working schedules

- Insurance coverage for Drone Nation assignments

- Can work part time or simply whenever they like

- Submit hours electronically to client for approval

- Easy payment procedure

- Paid within 20 business days of approved hours

- Opportunity to display work through photos and videos

I'm sure you're thinking, *Wait a minute! I have had numerous classes on marketing and I have never seen this as a step in the marketing strategy process. Why are we building a business model?* A high-level business model helps you clearly identify your target market, in the case of Drone Nation it helps you recognize that there are two target markets.

At least initially, Stan and Kristi will want to build a separate marketing strategy for each

1) Agriculture Drone Pilots

2) Potential Clients

Ok, so we are now going to build two separate marketing strategies for Drone Nation. Since the product is Drone Pilots we have to first build a marketing plan that will attract Drone Pilots to our site. We want them to sign up to provide our services. We do this first so that our clients will have a product to purchase, i.e. Certified Drone Pilots.

Note - As of Sept. 2017, the FAA had issued over 35,000 remote pilot certificates, according to an FAA spokesperson at the 2017 InterDrone conference.

Drone Pilots - Marketing Plan:

First, we have to build the basics:

- Website with links to all social media tools and matching email ids, keep it simple but professional
- Facebook page, when a pilot goes to your website or Facebook page they need to see a professional company that they want representing them and their services
- Marketing Plan Step 1 – Finding and Recruiting your Product, Professional Agriculture Drone Pilots
- Stan and Kristi have wisely chosen to focus on a layered plan that goes from "Very Specific" to a much broader "Non-Specific" marketing campaign.

Very specific is doing the upfront research necessary to build a Marketing Database of Remote Pilots with Names, Certifications, Expiration Dates, Agriculture Skills and History, Physical Addresses, Emails, Phone Numbers, and Websites where applicable and market directly to those Pilots. Well, that sounds good but where do we find FAA Certified Drone Pilots? In today's social media world, the answer is everywhere.

Let's start with the FAA, go to:

https://www.faa.gov/licenses_certificates/airmen_certification/releasable_airmen_download/

- Select "Airmen Certification" then
- Select "Database in Comma Separated Format (csv)" and download the database. It will download into a very large excel file
- This file contains all Pilots, not just Drone Pilots
- Sort by Rating and then delete everyone that is not U/SUAS rated. This will give you a list of approximately 30,000 Certified Pilots' names along with certifications and expiration dates
- You now have the start of your Marketing Database but you still have lots of work ahead of you and lots of blanks to fill in. The FAA also has a database of Pilots names and addresses for those pilots that have allowed the FAA to publish their address, cross reference your Drone pilot database to the address database and you

should now have about 10,000 Drone Pilots addresses to add to your growing database. Ok, were making progress but still lots to do

Next up is LinkedIn:

If you don't have a LinkedIn membership then sign up as it is an excellent recruiting tool for Drone Nation. As of this writing when I searched on "Drone Pilot" I had 8,265 hits. Send an invitation and an introductory message to all 8,265 and update your database accordingly. Time consuming but worth the effort, create a compelling message and then simply copy it into the invitation, this will save time and increase your connections to your target market.

- If you want to invest more time you will find hundreds of Drone Pilots have posted their resumes online.

- Go to Google and search on "Drone Pilot Resume". Once you get past the sample resume sites you will find hundreds of professional pilots; time to update your database. Let's say you now have 1,000 Pilot names and physical addresses and 6,000 more pilot emails. It's time to start the "specific" marketing portion of the campaign.

- Utilize mass mailing and emailing campaigns to recruit pilots to your site. Have a way for pilots to upload samples of their work to your YouTube site. Find ways to pull them in and make them part of the Drone Nation family.

- Do *something, anything, diffe* your competitors to attract pilots. to get creative.

Now for the Non-Specific marketing strategy. This is to find and recruit pilots that you don't have specific detailed access to.

- Attend Drone conferences as a speaker and panelist
- Start a local meeting group for Certified Commercial Drone Pilots, if one already exists in your area then join and attend the meetings
- Social Media, use Instagram, Facebook, YouTube, Twitter and others as appropriate
- Stay active posting on social media
- Post your pilots work even before they have been hired by a client, solicit photos and videos of their work for display on your Website and Facebook page. Most are proud of what they do and will be happy to share their work. Other prospective pilots will see this and be attracted to your team.
- If your client will allow you to share the finished product then share it online along with positive client comments. It's important to look larger than you are from the very beginning; the look and feel of success will attract both pilots and clients.
- Finally, Stan and Kristi will need to study their competitors to see what they have done in the way of marketing. As we said earlier, there is nothing wrong with learning from

others' success; just make sure the competitor you are learning from is successful.

What would we advise Stan and Kristi to do? Start Small, *Pick a Niche*. As an example, since Stan is already in the farming business, pick Agricultural Mapping as the niche. Attract pilot's specific to agriculture. Once they make this work, then expand to a second niche such as surveying. There is a lot to be said for starting small and making a business work before attempting to dig a 100 foot mine in search of a gold strike.

So, a quick review - Marketing consists of:

- Making your target market aware of your product
- Convincing them to buy your product
- Convincing them to buy your product again and again

When you first open your doors, your biggest challenge may be separating your marketing needs from your marketing wants. Capital is usually lean when you're just starting out, but now more than ever, there's not a dollar (nor a minute) to be wasted. Sure, it would be great to hear your company's advertisement on the local radio station or to see your company on a billboard on a well-traveled highway. But as we all know, these avenues of marketing are expensive, and they take time to develop. You need to project the image of your company and promote your product even before you open your doors. You need a starting point, in other words, and it needs to be effective and inexpensive.

In today's digital era, one of your top marketing tools is your web site. The latest statistics show that approximately 75% of the U.S. population uses the Internet, and that number is growing every day. There are lots of web design firms who would be happy to take your money, and lots of it, but establishing a web site can actually be quite inexpensive. You can have a web site up and running for under $1,000 by using a template; there are plenty of template sites that you can easily find on the Internet. The advantage of this type of web site is that it can be done easily, quickly, and inexpensively. The downside is that if you need a complex site, such as one that will allow your customers to interact with you, this route may not cut it for you.

Whether you modify an already-existing site or hire a web designer to build one from scratch, you need to do some homework. You'll have to make some decisions about how people will use your site—is it needed mainly for appearances, to signal that you are a professional, stable business, or does your business depend upon drone clients finding you on the Net? If it's the latter, then you definitely want a web site that will come up at the top of the list when people type your key words into a search engine. If you were a ranch photographer, for example, then you want your site designed such that it will emerge at the top of the list when people "Google" the words "ranch, survey, photography, your city, etc." If you only use your web site for identification purposes and as part of your image, you may not need that kind of response to a search engine inquiry. Making this decision up front will help you know what kind of web designer to contract. If you're going to depend on lots of web traffic for business, then spending a little extra on a great web designer and an SEO (search engine optimizer) will be more than worth it for you. Whatever type of site you have, come up with a URL address that's easy to remember, easy to type, and easy to say. This will help people in remembering it and remembering your company, and just naturally make it more notable.

This brings us to one word of caution: web sites are necessary, but don't assume that having a web site is an instant path to success. There is a prevailing misconception about what web sites can do for your company. Here's the truth: a web site won't create business by itself. It has to be combined with a massive dose of social marketing requiring tons of hours.

A good way to generate web traffic and market your business is through link swapping. Find companies that are not competitors but are complementary to your business and see if you can swap links with them. You place a link that goes to your web site on their front page and in return they get a link of the same size on your front page. You can engage in link swapping as often as it makes sense to do it. It's a win-win for everyone, and it costs nothing.

Next up are e-mail flyers. On a scale of 1-10 for inexpensive and effective, e-mail flyers get a 10. You can reach innumerable people very quickly especially if you have been able to build a specific list of potential clients, and it costs you virtually nothing. Develop a monthly e-mail flyer that will help keep current clients up to speed on your latest products, services, and sales. This is a great way to stay in touch with clients and to grow your business. Keep the flyer fun and entertaining—find a way in every issue to make the recipients smile; make your clients want to open the next flyer as soon as it arrives in their inbox. Keep the printed words to a minimum and include photos (people love photos). E-mail flyers cost next to nothing and once you have the flyer built you just change the content each month and send it back out. The only cost is time and once you've established that first flyer, your time is minimal. Remember to always leave your clients an easy way to opt out of receiving the flyer.

Likewise, build an e-mail distribution list, a LinkedIn page and Facebook page to disseminate notices about new products and/or forthcoming services, or go a step further and create an electronic newsletter. Make it a regular item and be persistent. A few people will ask to be unsubscribed from the list, but for the most part people respond positively, and you can provide a ton of information this way. Without a fee, you can capture e-mail IDs from trade shows, interest sign-up sheets at your store, and existing client e-mail IDs. When designing your newsletter, try and come up with an interesting format and something that makes yours different. Something as simple as providing a link to a live video that demonstrates your Drone capabilities can make an overwhelming difference.

The Internet has provided countless opportunities for marketing, far more than we can cover in this chapter. You can easily become connected with thousands of people and never leave your desk. Professional and social networking services such as LinkedIn, Facebook, and Twitter can connect you with people around the world, and many provide free basic levels of service. Blogs can also serve to get the word out about you and your business. Explore all your options. There's a world of free marketing out there to be had.

Now let's leave the digital world for a moment and talk about good old-fashioned print and television media. We know what some of you are thinking: *Hey wait, weren't we talking about free and low-cost marketing??* It's absolutely true that newspaper, magazine, and television ads can be expensive, but guess what? There are ways to make use of low-cost or even free print and television advertising. Inquire about remnant space advertising. When media outlets don't sell all of their advertising space or time before deadline, this "remnant" space or time can usually be bought at a deeply discounted price. And believe it or not, it is possible to find free media advertising, too. Many newspapers, for instance, have Focus sections that profile new businesses and business owners. Go online to your locals and see what their offerings are. Contact the newspaper and ask what they look for in determining whom to spotlight and whom to pass by. Get their attention in a way that fits their guidelines and be persistent until you land an interview. When the reporter comes out to interview you and preview your business, the article will be free . . . and priceless!

You can go about getting articles in local business magazines in the same way. Be proactive. Get an article written about yourself and your business, and with any luck you'll land on the front cover. This kind of exposure reaps a great deal of business, and again, it's absolutely free. There are also web-based services available to help you distribute your story to business magazines and newspapers [PRWeb is a good example].

Of course, if you have a truly unique line of business or if you do something really extraordinary, newspapers, magazines, and television stations may come calling you. This is free advertising at its best!

Once you do get into a newspaper or magazine or on television news, follow up with the reporter or any other contacts you made in the process. Stay in touch with them just as if they were a client: include them on your monthly e-mail flyer, mailing list, newsletter, and so on and *Always build relationships wherever you go.*

At some point early in the planning process, you'll need to devise a company logo. Company logos are a very visual way to get people's attention. There are thousands of design firms who would be happy to take your money and create a customized design, but if you simply don't have the money, look no further than your local university's art or design department. You can contract with a college student to develop a logo that satisfies your needs. These kids are creative, and they're technology- and media-savvy. They'll work for much less than established design firms, and you'll be doing them a favor by putting a little money in their pocket and giving them some real-world experience.

One terrific way to build relationships and get the word out about your company is to attend trade shows and conferences. Participating in trade shows can be expensive, but you can benefit from them initially for very little money by being an attendee only. You'll have an opportunity to talk to hundreds of people and get the word out about your company. Collect and exchange business cards as you go and use them throughout the year to follow up on opportunities. The real benefit of trade shows and conferences is the relationships you develop with potential clients at the breakout sessions and interest seminars.

Certainly, there are other ways to maximize the benefit of trade shows. Approximately nine to ten months before a trade show occurs, the company producing it will be looking for speakers. Submit a proposal and use that speaking opportunity to further your networking and to promote your company services and/or products. You can also find a fellow entrepreneur whose business complements yours and negotiate the opportunity to participate at little or no cost to yourself. If you are a participant, collect business cards for a free giveaway. Instead of blindly drawing a name out of the business card pot, select a name and gain an appointment with the person who "won" to expand your business opportunity.

A word to the wise. Trade shows aren't for all companies but visiting them as a guest and not a participant will give you the opportunity to determine if they should be part of your marketing plan. We've actually had mixed results with trade shows. Why? Because the Drone environment is a very crowded field. Herein lies an important marketing lesson: when you are a commodity, conferences and trade shows will provide little to no value to your bottom line. Once you add a unique service, conferences become a very valuable marketing source, worth the investment dollars. Just keep in mind that participating in trade shows is not economical unless it brings you business.

Some of the best marketing you can do is coming up with something unique to your company to advertise what you do. As a new entrepreneur you will be plagued with contact from advertising companies who have marvelous ways to spend your money. If you can do something a little different than the standard mug or ballpoint pen, something that stands out, something that reflects your company's spirit of adventure. Find something about your company that is unique—or that can become unique—and use it as part of your marketing program.

If you're looking for more unusual ideas for marketing, another is to have a company vehicle "wrapped" with a design that gains attention and gets the word out about your business. The wrap costs relatively little and gives you advertising wherever you go! The wrap should feature your company name and logo and your web site. It can easily be removed when the vehicle is sold or your marketing program changes. At the very least, any company vehicle should feature your logo and a way to get in touch with you. If you don't have a company vehicle, consider advertising on your personal vehicle. The cost of a small sign is nominal, and it brings you lots of exposure.

Now let's shift our discussion to some more of the nuts-and-bolts elements of your marketing campaign. How about your company collateral? Company collateral—all the print media associated with your business—is necessary to run a good business and is a terrific form of marketing. Brochures, flyers, newsletters, invoices, pamphlets, and all the other printed materials you use are all important parts of providing clients and potential clients with information about what you do. There are plenty of companies who'd love to design and print everything from your brochures to your letterhead to your mailing labels. If money is tight, invest in a color printer and generate your initial company collateral yourself. With the technology available today, you'll be amazed at what you can turn out with a limited amount of time and money. Printing your own company collateral is also an inexpensive way to find out what works and what doesn't. Spending a sizable amount of money upfront for collateral is money that cannot be recouped if it turns out you missed!

Then, when the time arrives to have your brochures and other print media created professionally, don't print things that might change such as your address, managers' names, phone number, temporary promotional campaigns, or other specific data on the outside team. Instead, utilize individual handout sheets that provide specifics and design them in such a way that you can reprint only one instead of the entire brochure. Having to create the entire brochure or pamphlet every time you make a change is incredibly expensive. Think of it as a menu-driven document and prepare sections as separate handouts that can be pulled and exchanged with others. Our first collateral was completely printed in-house. Later, when we had the money we switched to professionally printed brochures. We now have covers professionally printed with no specific data on them and we fill the inside with individual flyers that we print and are tailored to a client's specific interests. This is the best of both worlds and it keeps our cost to a minimum.

Satisfied customers, of course, also provide free marketing for your company. Word-of-mouth remains the best marketing tool by far. People are usually more than happy to pass along recommendations, and you want to make sure your clients are satisfied and that they will be able to give you a great review on the spot.

Don't ever hesitate to simply ask people for marketing ideas, too. Most people enjoy being creative, and they'll be flattered that you asked for their input. Certainly, there are creative people within your own team, but also seek outside ideas from friends, family, and where appropriate, even other business associates—you never know when someone will come up with a brilliant idea that will pay off.

Get creative yourself. Once you start your own business, you'll find that your brain will just be full of new business ideas. Write them down for later consideration—sometimes these ideas will be something you can incorporate into your current business as a new product line or maybe you could turn up a great marketing idea. Our experience with marketing is that when we were creative and did it ourselves, we tended to get better results. And, we saved money!

Whatever your marketing strategy, remember that marketing is a long-term, dig-in-your-heels endeavor. You've got to learn what works and what does not, and that takes time. You'll also discover that you may need to redirect your marketing strategies as your company evolves. There will never be a day when you aren't engaged in some sort of marketing, and if you're savvy about it, you'll create ideas and strategies that will serve you for the long run. Business cards, brochures, and items like the Drone paperweights stay on people's desks or in their files indefinitely. We've had instances of new clients contacting us based upon some marketing item they'd kept for as long as four years before they acted upon it!

When we launched Argus Rising we budgeted very little for marketing. We looked for every opportunity we could find to assist us in getting our name known on social media, and to this day we still look for those same opportunities. Legitimate free marketing is not difficult to find; you just have to invest some time in looking for it. Free or low-cost social marketing lets you hit the ground running when your "natural resources" are scarce, and it gives you the chance to take advantage of different marketing formats that will help you understand what works and what does not work for your business. Your only investment is time. Once you find a marketing format that has a positive return you won't mind investing the money. And why would you? It will be money that returns to you again and again.

Chapter Three Notes:
Marketing
On a Shoestring

- Every successful business needs an effective marketing campaign. You need creative ways to advertise your product or service, convince customers to buy your product or service, and convince them to buy again and again.
- There are plenty of effective marketing ideas that cost little or even nothing. Some of our best marketing ideas are things we devised ourselves and produced in-house.
- Remember that marketing is a long-term endeavor; there will never come a time when you do not need to market your business. Be prepared to change your marketing plan as needed.
- In review, within this chapter, we have provided twenty effective marketing ideas; find what works best for you.

CHAPTER FOUR
There are Lots of Miners
Do Something, Anything, Differently

No matter what line of Drone business you select, you will likely encounter many other Miners with the same idea and if not, there will be soon. So, what's a miner to do? Simple, create your competitive advantage by doing *something, anything, differently*. You may not see many others in your selected field but the time to think long-term is right now, before you even open your doors. One of the most effective things you can do to ensure your business's long-term survival is to create a competitive advantage by having a unique niche in the industry. For Argus Rising this was focusing on and building our class material specifically for First Responders. There are lots of drone training companies and they will train first responders but to date no one can compete with our class syllabus built specifically for first responders. Your ability to build a competitive advantage in any business is one of the most crucial steps that you must pass through to becoming a successful entrepreneur.

We set out to build a Drone Training company unlike any before it, but how could we possibly do that? There are lots of Drone training companies. How then could we provide a training service that would be unlike any other Drone training company's out there? The challenge before us was simple—we had to *do something, anything, differently!*

We also knew we had to start with the very foundation of the company or any change would be too insignificant to make a difference. We already had a firm idea of our foundation, and if you've paid attention at all, you know what it is—people. Our goal was to attract seasoned Aviation Professionals, First Responders and Military Veterans as course developers and instructors. To do this we modeled our previous company, using the same values we did then. It's a value system with a proven track record that will provide outstanding results that your competitors can not improve upon. It reflects how you run your business from the top to the bottom and vice versa. Capture your values in writing and be sure that each of your employees understands and demonstrates those values every day.

Consistently Superior Performance – Argus employees and associates are held to a higher standard. Their personal commitment to performance is reflected in every action taken. Argus employees understand the expectations and exceed them on a daily basis. Employees are encouraged to run with the team, share their ideas, and always be proactive.

Attitude, Attitude, Attitude – No one cares how much you know until they know how much you care. We believe attitude, teamwork and the ability to truly enjoy your work are requirements to being successful.

Professionalism and Pride – We are a professional organization and we expect that standard to be reflected in everything, from the way employees dress to the quality of their work. Employees should take pride in their work and company, injecting quality into everything they do.

Respect for Each Other – We are all different and we celebrate our differences; they are what make us interesting. A lack of respect for any individual in the form of sexual harassment or racially-/religiously-motivated comments or actions will not be tolerated and will be grounds for immediate dismissal. We set our standards high and we expect all employees to do the same.

Ethics – A decision made by any Argus employee should be able to withstand the "in the light of day" test. If your decision were printed in tomorrow's headlines "in the light of day," would it cause embarrassment or concern? If so, you need to rethink your decision. Ethical judgment is to be used in all actions.

These simple Core Values set us apart from other companies from the minute we opened our doors. We took what should be the basic foundation for any company and put our signature on the bottom of it. These values clearly send the message that Argus is a company that can be trusted.

Okay, so now that we had all the elements of the right foundation in place, it was time to brainstorm how we were actually going to do business differently. What we wanted from the outset was a *long-term* strategy for success. As we've already seen, too many start-ups are initially fueled on passion alone, and while passion and enthusiasm are essential for getting a business off the ground, they won't ensure your long-term survival. But guess what? Doing *something, anything, differently* directly impacts your chances of

long-term success. In our experience, the strategy for long-term success requires three basic things:
1. Building a Competitive Advantage
2. Maximizing your Profit
3. Investing in the Future

Let's look at each part of the strategy in turn and see how doing *something, anything, differently* contributes to each one.

Build a Competitive Advantage

Building a competitive advantage is all about doing *something, anything, differently.* Can you provide a truly unique Drone service or product, something that no one else offers? If so you can skip this section, as you have no competitors, or at least not at the moment!

We're guessing, however, that like most business owners, you're one among many providing the same or very similar products and services, and that you need to devise ways to distinguish yourself from your competition. Now, it goes without saying that you should always strive to provide a superior product or service and superior customer service—one of the surest ways to out-do your competition and remain in the game for the long run is to deliver consistently superior results and cultivate strong customer relations. What we want to discuss here is how doing *something, anything, differently* actually created our competitive advantage.

From the outset, we worked to build one-on-one relationships with our First Responders, we take the time to understand their individual issues, and design classes tailored to their individual needs. And do you know what happened? Our clients loved it. What client wouldn't? What client wouldn't want to feel as though their needs were being individually heard, assessed, and met? It seems like a no-brainer to tailor a particular class to fit a particular requirement, but this is something that just wasn't happening when we launched Argus Rising, and it gave us our competitive advantage. What's more, it's *still* giving us our competitive advantage. From this input we have developed advance classes specific to First Responders such as Search and Rescue, Active Shooter and Crime Scene Recreation just to name a few. This is exactly where Argus has a competitive advantage over its competitors. We are much more nimble, flexible, and quick than many of the other training companies and we have the time and resources to pour much more energy into cultivating relationships.

Our company model didn't stop there, however. It actually changed the way we did everything. We wanted to make sure that our new model started at the top, so the way executive management led the company would be different. The root of our leadership style grows right out of our people-focused company culture. When we hear good comments about one of our people from a client, that comment is acknowledged and passed on to the individual and the team. When work requires that a team works on a problem all night, we are there dropping off pizza and cheering them on. Our people are directly responsible for the Argus success story and our management style reflects that fact.

Our executive management teams are expected to lead with the same eye to putting people first. Our efforts may seem extreme to some but remember that we do not manufacture a product or have any significant assets—our assets are our people and we never forget that.

Our model affects how we train field people, too. We recognize that people skills are as important as technical skills, so along with technical training, we send instructors to classes that focus on communications skills, interpersonal skills, and relationship skills. Our clients know nobody will work harder than Argus to solve their problems. Our executive management motto is simple: "Work Hard and Play Hard." It's the distillation of how to do business and reflects back to the original Argus Connection.

In short, we built a business model that was better than what was out there. Thus, not only did we create an improved model that better served clients, we differentiated ourselves from our competitors and made a name for ourselves.

There's one final thing you should know about defining your business. Business may require that you be willing to redefine your business multiple times if necessary. A good idea only lasts so long, after all, and if you want to stay in business you must keep up with the demands of the market. There's always a new competitive advantage to be found. Always be prepared to do *something, anything, differently*!

Maximize Your Profit

The next step in building long-term success is simple once you grasp the full measure of the concept, and that is to *maximize your profit on every engagement.*

In business the perceived value of something is directly associated with its price. So, if you give something away for free, its perceived value is zero. Likewise, a high-end price point signals consumers that your product is worth the money. Your aim is to establish a price point that is high enough that it signals a high value, but low enough not to scare away consumers. You need to find a price point that will ensure a profit for your business.

Is there such a thing as too much profit? Companies such as IBM and Microsoft, who maximize profit on every engagement, will tell you no and here's why.

Let's take a look at Trevor's Drone Store in Small Town, USA selling drones and all things related to Drones. Trevor rented space in a local strip mall and has an online presence for shoppers. Trevor calculates his monthly bills, payroll, and his expected average sales and then makes sure that his prices reflect those expenses and a few additional dollars for unexpected business events. Trevor is not looking to get rich and even though he knows he could get a few more dollars on each drone sale he keeps his prices low—these are, after all, his customers, and he has built a loyal following.

What's going on here? Trevor doesn't yet know that he needs to be maximizing profit on every engagement. What's going on is that Trevor is running an outstanding *short-term* business. It's short-term because Trevor does not understand long-term competitive forces. In plain English, "long-term competitive forces" means that there will always be a competitor looking to put you out of business. There will always be a competitor looking to create a competitive advantage and win the upper hand.

So, what is Trevor to do? He must maximize his profit on every engagement.

Let's start with what this does *not* mean. It does not mean ripping off your clients or overcharging because your client is not paying attention or abusing your vendors. Maximizing profit on every engagement also doesn't mean that you're engaging in corporate greed—it has nothing whatsoever to do with accumulating profit out of pure self-interest. Maximizing profit on every engagement allows Trevor to invest in the future and build a long-term competitive success model. Your objective is to capture the maximum dollar your client is willing to pay while minimizing what you invested in bringing the product to market. The one qualifier, and this is key, is that your client must feel good about the exchange. Your client must feel that the purchase is a win-win situation not just today but tomorrow and six months from now or they will eventually suffer from buyer's remorse, and buyer's remorse will cause you to lose business.

Now, can you have low prices and still maximize profit? Absolutely! You have to remember that profit and revenue are not the same thing. It's common for businesses to mistake *revenue* (the total income produced) with *profit* (the money left after all expenditures). The lure of a multimillion-dollar deal will often mask the *real* bottom line, the profit. Profit is the difference between your cost and the sale price. Just look at Southwest Airlines if you want to see how to maximize profit and retain a low price point. Southwest focuses on lowering their cost and thus maximizing their profit. How does this work? Once an airline schedules a flight their cost is relatively fixed. In other words, their cost has little variance whether the plane has ten passengers or 100 passengers, therefore filling every seat has a great deal of value (profit) attached to it. The Southwest strategy is to reduce their cost and then keep fares low to encourage filling every seat, thus maximizing the profit of every scheduled flight. They then combine low fares with another competitive advantage of frontline people who actually enjoy being at work, and when you do that you have a winning combination in the airline industry.

The bottom line is that consistent sustainable profit is the driving force of a company. Without it, you won't survive for any appreciable length of time. Your focus must always be on how to maximize profit on every engagement, and you should be willing to walk away from unprofitable business. And by the way, never believe that a client will watch out for your interests in the area of profit, even if you know the client well and trust them—it's not the client's job to make sure you run a healthy business! If you've built a competitive advantage by doing *something, anything, differently* and if you continually strive to maximize profit, you're creating a strategy for long-term success. With these steps in place, it's time to plan for a long-term future.

Invest in the Future

Investing in the future, at its simplest, means that you're taking steps to ensure that your business will be around for years to come. Investing in the future requires that you're always finding new competitive advantages or strengthening the competitive advantages you have, and that you're maximizing profit on every engagement. It requires that you sharpen your business model continually, that you're relentless in looking for ways to improve it. If you must redefine your business ten times in order to stay in business for the long run, then that's what you have to do to invest in your future. The tendency is to find a business model that works and think, *Aha! I found it – I can do this for the next 20 years!* But the truth is you can't. You won't even make it the next twenty months before a competitor finds a way to do it better. Therefore, you have to be constantly aware of market trends and customer needs. You must also be constantly aware of what your competition is up to. Investing in the future requires that you're cognizant of the fact that there is always someone who wants to put you out of business. This may sound paranoid but remember Andrea's observation: "The paranoid survive."

The specific steps a business will take to invest in its future will be particular to each individual business, but in broad terms, investing in the future consists of:

1. Planning a profit model that allows you to be in the game for the long run
2. Listening to your clients so you understand their current needs and can anticipate their future needs
3. Staying abreast of industry and market trends and attending conferences to evaluate new ideas
4. Building and maintaining relationships with your key clients

5. Constantly looking for ways to do *something, anything, differently,* and when you find a new solution that makes sense, investing in it

Now let's return to our old pal Trevor, Trevor is in the drone retail business in a town that doesn't have any drone outlets. If Trevor had a crystal ball and could look into the future, what do you think he would see? You got it—drones in every big box retail from Walmart to Best Buy providing prices that he simply cannot compete with. How many stories have we heard of the small-town retail shops being put of business by the big box stores? It's not as if it is hard to see this future, what's tough is figuring out what Trevor does about it. The answer is simple – Trevor has to invest in the future. But what does that mean? Trevor can't possibly compete with price or selection against a national model. What Trevor has to do is *something, anything, differently,* and that requires creative thinking and investment dollars. Here's one version of Trevor's strategy for investing in the future:

- Trevor needs to spend serious time studying his competitors. He needs to walk the aisles of their store and become thoroughly familiar with their prices and their selection. He needs to know the hours they're open, how their people handle customers, are they knowledgeable about drones, how their management team leads, and so on—he needs to gather all the data he can.
- Ultimately, Trevor needs to assess his data. The advantages the big box retailer offers are easy for him to see, but what he must focus on are their disadvantages. Trevor jots down a list:

- o Poor to mediocre service – employees were difficult to find, and when I asked a drone related question, it took three different people to give a reasonable answer
- o Size - it is time-consuming to find what you need
- o Poor atmosphere – the friendly, feel-good atmosphere of my store is non-existent at the big store; one could easily spend half an hour in the store and not have an employee say hello

Trevor's investment in the future and strategy for long-term success is becoming clearer. He needs to invest in people who are committed to making the business successful, committed to building relationships with the clients, committed to providing service and knowledge beyond anyone's expectations, committed to knowing exactly where every nut and bolt is, and committed to understanding "how to" so they can assist customers with questions and solutions. In short, Trevor needs to invest in employees who will go the extra mile in building customer relationships; his employees need to know every return client's name and go out of their way to make a client feel welcome and assisted. Then Trevor needs to build an atmosphere that makes customers feel good from the moment they walk into his store. He needs frontline help that can point a customer to the exact department they need, reducing the amount of time it requires to find what they're after.

And from a purely numbers standpoint, Trevor needs to expand his on-line offerings and a purchase storage warehouse so he can take advantage of bulk purchases to keep his pricing within a reasonable range of the big corporations. And guess what? Trevor can't do any of the above without maximizing his profit and investing in the future. Don't ever think you can't compete with the big boys. You can! You just have to figure out their weaknesses and then make those weaknesses your strengths.

Doing *something, anything, differently* is one of the best means to success we know of. It distinguishes you from your competition and gives you a competitive advantage, it helps you remain on top of market trends and consumer needs, it contributes to your bottom line, and it allows you to invest in the future. Sometimes, doing something differently is a gradual process that occurs over many months or even years. But the far more likely scenario is that you'll be faced with major business decisions that must be acted upon within days. You must be prepared to utilize new ideas or a competitive advantage at a moment's notice—if you don't, your competition will!

Chapter Four Notes:
There are Lots of Miners
Do Something, Anything, Differently

- You must always be on the lookout for how to do *something, anything, differently*. Doing something differently will create a niche in the market for your business and will distinguish you from your competition.
- In defining what you will do differently, you must review the old standards that have been forgotten or neglected and then add new creative ideas without worrying about traditional boundaries. Do your homework and plan for every contingency, but never be afraid of striking out into wholly new territory.
- The strategy for long-term success consists of 1) building a competitive advantage 2) maximizing profit and 3) investing in your future. Doing *something, anything, differently* contributes to each step in the process.
- Look to your competition to see where you can build a competitive advantage. Is there something you can do better than they do? Can you offer a solution they don't? Or, do you need to totally redefine your business to create that competitive advantage? Be prepared to redefine your business multiple times if necessary.
- Consistent sustainable profit is the lifeblood of a business. Without it, you simply won't survive.

CHAPTER FIVE
Architecting Your Gold Mine –
Beyond the Business Plan

You have staked your claim and done your homework and it's time to document a "Business Plan" for your personal Drone Business. In this chapter we're going to focus on something most how-to books don't tell you about: the true role a business plan should play in getting your business off the ground, and your ability to look beyond it if need be—even to the point that you end up with a radically different business than you had originally envisioned.

Now hold on, don't get nervous! We're not saying that you should be prepared to transform your Drone services business into a used car dealership, or even that such a transformation is likely. Our point is that if they *had* to, the successful gold miners of the business world could adapt to even the wildest of curveballs—recession, loss of key employees, new market trends, unanticipated setbacks, unforeseen opportunities, you name it. By all means you should come up with a solid business plan, which is utterly necessary both for you and your investors, but here's a little fact that the how-to books seldom mention: relying <u>solely</u> on a plan will lead to failure. A business plan is rarely a road map of how your business is actually going to happen. You will quickly find that when plans meet reality it is not reality that will yield, it is your plan. As much as we'd like to predict the future and chart a path of steady upward growth, a business plan is not your day-to-day guide to success. Instead, it's best to think of it as *an overview of only one possible outcome.* If you're smart you won't hesitate to change the plan when a better opportunity or idea presents itself, or when you discover that your original business plan just isn't going to work. If you're like most entrepreneurs, you don't want to believe that your business plan could prove unfeasible, but guess what? It happens all the time. Successful entrepreneurs don't let this stop them. They are able to take what at first appears to be a setback or an insurmountable challenge and turn it into even greater opportunity. We're going to tell you two such stories below.

But first, let's do something fun. (Hey, who said work wasn't fun?) We're going to do an exercise together, and it's not going to take any more effort than to let your imagination run wild. So, find a quiet spot, relax, close your eyes, put your feet up—do whatever you have to do to prepare yourself to get creative. Now imagine yourself in the future. We'll start with three years from now. What do you want to be doing? Honesty is key. Don't let outside influences answer the question for you. It may be all too apparent where your spouse, business partner, parent, or current boss wants you to be in three years, but this time is just for you. Don't put limitations on yourself, either. If you want to be running a multimillion-dollar business in three years, dream big. Okay, so in the best of all possible worlds, what do you see yourself doing? Whatever your goal is, document it. Write it down at the top of a piece of paper, in large capital letters.

Let's say you want a home-based Drone service business, and you want a personal annual income of $100,000. Now think of that two-pronged goal as a point on a map, a destination. For the purpose of this exercise we'll nickname that place "Austin." (Hey, why not? People from all over the world and every background love Austin!) Whatever your "Austin" is, this is where you personally want to go, and you have three years to get there.

Now stay in creativity mode, because next you need to understand why you want to get there. *Why* do you want to go Austin? Fill in the blanks, as many as you need. I want to go Austin because...

1._____

2._____

3._____

4._____

5._____

Maybe your answers are 1) Financial freedom 2) I'm passionate about drones 3) I want to use my skills professionally, not just as a hobby 4) I want to be my own boss 5) I don't want to be stuck behind a desk all day. Write down whatever is true for you. When we've done this exercise with people, we've seen everything from *I want to set my own hours* to *I want to make enough money to pay for my grandkids' education* to *I can't spend another day in my cube* to *I want to set an example of success for my children.* One guy even said he wanted to start a home-based business so he could spend more time with his dog. Hey, whatever gets you ready to conquer the day!

You now know where you want to go and why you want to go there. The final questions to be answered are:

1. How badly do you want to arrive at this destination? In answering this one, don't just say "really bad." Think about what you're willing to give and what you're willing to give up to get to Austin.
2. Does this destination create excitement and enthusiasm when you talk about it to others? Sure, you're excited, but can you communicate your vision to others in such a way that *they* get excited?
3. Are you motivated to get out of bed every morning ready to execute this journey? Answer with unabashed honesty. Are you willing to do whatever it takes to make it to Austin even if the journey takes you into uncharted territory?

Write down all of your answers. What you're doing is formulating a *Goals Document*. Conventional wisdom says that your business plan is paramount, but guess what? Your Goals Document is just as important as the most well formulated of business plans.

Your Goals Document does not need to be formal or lengthy or even grammatically correct— unless you specifically want to share it, no one is going to see it except you. This is your personal document of what you want to achieve. Note that there is nothing in here relative to a business plan except perhaps the size of the business that you would like to own.

Getting to Austin now becomes your daily and weekly focus. We encourage people to set weekly, if not daily, goals on how they're going to get to Austin. This keeps you focused and motivated, and it provides some built-in accountability. In corporate America you answer to a hierarchy of management and there are pre-set objectives that must be met according to predetermined timelines. In the wild world of entrepreneurship, you're on your own. It's up to you and you alone to wake up ready to conquer the day and transport yourself to Austin. This is why a Goals Document is so important. We're all going to have days in which we feel as though Austin is unreachable and we want to give up. A review of your Goals Document should be enough to vanquish this temporary crisis of confidence and get you back mining for gold.

Let's look at an example. Let's say your business plan is to own a "Custom Drone" shop. You know the business and you've figured out a way to redefine it and you're ready to go. Your business plan is focused on "How to Run a Successful Custom Drone Shop" and might include market studies on other Drone business in the area, recent growth trends of the city, the first year's financials, and et cetera.

Now here's the key: your Drone shop is your vehicle for getting to Austin, it is not Austin itself. You might respond, "But I have a real passion for Drones!" That's great and that's why you chose the Drone shop as your business, but don't let the passion you feel for Drones and owning a Drone shop (something we hope you outlined in your Goals Document) obscure the fact that your Drone shop itself is merely the means to get you to your larger goal. In fact, when it comes right down to it, Austin and your Drone shop are unrelated.

Now what if you think, "This can't be! Drones are my passion and I want to operate the best custom-built Drone shop in the state. I'm sure the Drone shop is my Austin." Well, we love your enthusiasm and your commitment, but let us repeat: your Drone shop is *not* your Austin. This is certainly not to say that you shouldn't be passionate about your business, and in fact we encourage you to pick a business that you are passionate about. Just be sure you don't confuse the means to an end with the end itself.

Never make your final goal the business no matter how passionate you are about it. The business is the vehicle that will get you to Austin; Austin is your final goal. Let us put it another way. The business is the tangible result of all the effort you put in to reaching Austin; Austin is the sum total of all the intangible rewards that come as a result of the business. In the example we reviewed above, the Drone shop is the means by which you will reach Austin. What is Austin? It's everything recorded in your Goals Document: financial freedom, a passion for cooking, a desire to use your skills professionally, a desire to be your own boss, an aversion to being stuck behind a desk all day.

A real-life example will bring the point home, while this example is not Drone specific it does drive home the point. A gentleman we'll call Jeremiah grew up on a ranch with all sorts of animals, and he became passionate about rescuing and protecting wildlife. He worked a corporate job but kept his passion alive by volunteering with his local animal shelter and occasionally participating in national ASPCA and World Wildlife events and fundraisers. He made a good living, more than enough to support his family, but he was well aware that his job was just a job—it hardly came close to fulfilling his passion. When eventually he inherited his family's 240-acre ranch, Jeremiah saw a perfect opportunity to pursue his lifelong passion. Part of the land would be used as an animal sanctuary; to make money he would establish an educational center where people could come to learn about and observe animals in their natural habitat. So, Jeremiah worked up a business plan and presented it to the bank. The bank was willing to finance him using the land as collateral, and Jeremiah resigned from corporate America, moved his family to the ranch, and opened his center.

Two years later the business was struggling to stay afloat, the ranch was mortgaged to the hilt, and his passion for rescuing animals had been worn thin by the daily grind of trying to make the business successful and take care of his family. Then, as if he needed any more salt in an already painful wound, he discovered that his fence was down in the lower forty acres; motorcycle tracks covered the surrounding hills. He repaired the fence and posted No Trespassing signs and went on about his business, but week after week he would find a section of fence down and multiple new tracks.

It was about this time that we met Jeremiah. Among other things, we discussed with him the different roles a Goals Document and a business plan play in a successful business, and we were not surprised to find that he had not formulated a Goals Document. We led him through the process, and Jeremiah quickly saw that over the two years he had been in business for himself, he had lost sight of his original goals and confused the actual business with his Austin. When he saw the difference, he realized that he needed a vehicle, any vehicle, to get to Austin, which in his case was rescuing and protecting animals. In the end, here's the essence of what he came up with in his Goals Document:

- <u>Goal</u> - In three years I want to be running a business with revenues of $1 million-plus and a personal income in excess of $150,000 per year.
- <u>Why?</u> – So that I can have the financial independence to focus on rescuing animals in need while making a good living for my family. When it is all said and done, rescuing animals is what I want to do with my life, which is my Austin.

Deep down, Jeremiah's passion and his original goals were still alive. It took only one conversation for him to remember what he wanted to accomplish and where his passion and enthusiasm lay. The problem was that over time, his focus had shifted from getting to Austin to getting through the day-to-day grind of running a failing business. What he now realized was that the business he'd started with the best of intentions (not to mention a solid business plan) was not Austin itself, and it was not going to get him to Austin.

So, what happened? After working through his Goals Document and not focusing on his business plan to the exclusion of all else, Jeremiah saw an opportunity. He decided to work with what was right there in front of his nose. He used what was left of the bank financing to grade the forty acres so popular with the "trespassers" with additional hills and challenging banks, and he opened an incredibly successful off-road motocross track. Jeremiah has now accomplished his original goals:

- At the end of three years he was running a full-time business with revenues exceeding

$1 million and a personal income in excess of $150,000 per year.

- He now has the financial independence to focus on rescuing animals and he makes enough to take care of his family. In fact, Jeremiah was so successful that he was able to purchase 200 adjoining acres, more than making up for the forty-acre diminishment of the sanctuary land.

Jeremiah's vehicle for getting to Austin was not the one he expected or planned on, but when all is said and done, Jeremiah has made it to Austin. He has accomplished what he wanted to do with his life. Without shifting his focus from his business plan to his goals he may have never strayed from his original business plan, and in all likelihood, would have spent years struggling with a business that in the end would falter and die.

One last question remains. Why did the bank loan Jeremiah money if he had a bad business plan? It didn't, and Jeremiah didn't have a bad business plan. The bank loaned him money against his ranch, and even though they reviewed his business plan, they could have cared less about his ability to succeed. The plan didn't get him the loan, the collateral did. When Jeremiah walked out the bank door his business plan went into the circular file. Never expect anyone on the outside of your business to protect you from bad decisions!

With Argus Rising our goal was to become actively engaged in a people-oriented business that would reap us relationship and financial benefits as we move towards what most people consider retirement years. It's always fun working with a team of totally focused and talented individuals. Our desire was to create an environment where a creative team would excel in the Drone business.

So, we had our goals documented and our business plan in place, we knew the difference between Austin itself and the vehicle that would get us there, and we understood the training sector. What happened when the rubber hit the road and we opened our doors? Remember how we said that a business plan is rarely a plan of how a business would actually proceed?

Our original plan was to provide top-quality training services to commercial pilots. Roughly speaking, "training" comes in the form of long-term and short-term projects. A good example of long-term project would be to train Drone pilots for a business such as Amazon. An example of a short-term training project is a 5-day Bootcamp for individuals wishing to use Drones commercially. It was not long before we were running a brisk business. In other words, we were well on our way to Austin.

Then, wouldn't you know it, we got our equivalent of motocross drivers trespassing in our lower forty acres!

We were approached by a local detective and asked if we could provide First Responder training. He needed a tailored course specific to First Responders. The easy answer was "No" since we did not have the First Responder curriculum he was asking for and tailored curriculums are costly and time consuming. But eager to please our client and sensing a larger opportunity, our response was, "Absolutely! We would be happy to do that."

The truth was, we understood "training" backwards and forward, but the only thing we knew about First Responders was what we all see in the daily news. At the same time, we were open to exploring new territory, and we thought, *how hard could it be to develop what the detective was asking for and what value would it have after completion?* Without a moment's hesitation we were off and running.

We were honest with the detective upfront and told him we would have to develop the course, he had no issue with that as he would get the opportunity to have input into the final training course. So, we were off and running! The detective provided the input we needed to develop an amazing 5-Day First Responder course complete with numerous missions that would likely challenge them in their near future. And then guess what happened? It wasn't long before we got another request for the course, and then a third and a fourth. Though first responder training wasn't part of our original business plan, we were always focused on commercial training, we weren't about to let a prime opportunity to help us get to Austin pass us by. That's how the current "Argus Rising" was born. We learned how to teach First Responders, developed Advanced First Responder Courses such as Search and Rescue, Active Shooter, Active Fire, Active Crime Scene, Crime and Accident Scene Photography, Orthomosaics, Thermal Imaging, etc., specifically for First Responders.

Like Jeremiah's motocross business, first responder training was never part of our business plan. It was never even on our radar scope, and we knew next to nothing about that area of business. But because we were focused each day on our personal goals (i.e., on Austin) and not on a specific business plan, we were extremely flexible and open to any new opportunity that would get us to our Austin. If we had stubbornly stuck to our original business plan, we would've missed out on one of the most lucrative opportunities that ever came our way.

A Goals Document is an invaluable tool for getting you to Austin—it's just as important as a well-formulated business plan. A business plan is necessary, but a Goals Document will take you into the intangible reasons you wanted to pick up that nugget in the first place. Factors such as being one's own boss, enjoying the freedom and passion of the entrepreneurial adventure, or being financially independent are powerfully motivating. It's these life goals that get you out of bed ready to master the day; it's these goals that get you through the dark days of recession or setbacks; it's these goals that inspire you to persevere when you discover that your original business plan simply is not going to work. While a Goals Document is much simpler to create than a business plan, that doesn't mean it's any less important. You should put just as much emphasis on creating your personal Goals Document as your business plan. With a sound business plan and a thorough Goals Document, you've got a near-guaranteed ticket to your own personal Austin.

CHAPTER 5 NOTES:
Architecting Your Gold Mine
Beyond the Business Plan

- When planning your business, give as much priority and attention to your Goals Document as to your business plan. Your Goals Document takes you into the intangible reasons you wanted to go into business in the first place and contains powerful motivational tools that can get you through any difficulty.

- A business plan is rarely a road map of how your business will be run on a day-to-day guide to success. Rather, think of it as an outline of one possible outcome. Things rarely occur according to plan; be ready to adapt as necessary.

- In formulating your Goals Document, think of where you want to be in three years. What do you want to be doing? This is your own personal Austin.

- Then list all the reasons you want to get to Austin. Popular answers are financial independence, being your own boss, the thrill of entrepreneurship, and so on, but list your own personal answers. Be 100% honest.

- Make getting to Austin your personal mission. Your weekly and daily focus will be on getting to Austin.

- Your business will be the vehicle by which you get there. Never confuse Austin with your business itself!

- We can almost guarantee that your journey to Austin will take you on unexpected side trips and lead you down unexplored paths. Not to worry – this is all part of the entrepreneurial adventure! Be willing to look beyond your business plan and deviate from your original path. Remain open to unforeseen ways of getting to Austin.

Success Often Lies in Unexpected Opportunities

CHAPTER SIX

The Hunt for Start-up Capital
How Much and Where to Get It

The professional consultants will tell you that in general you shouldn't start a company without a minimum of $250,000 in investment capital. Hmmmm, we started our first company Argus Connection (A Multi-Million Dollar Corporation) on $10,000 and a credit card. Surely we could do the same with Argus Rising.

Two hundred and fifty thousand dollars! Wouldn't we all like to have a quarter of a million in investment capital for our first company? But let's face it, very, very few of us have access to that kind of up-front cash. Twenty years ago, we were in the same situation so many of you are in right now—we had the desire, we had the abilities and skills, we had the drive, but as far as start-up capital went we had next to nothing. Thus, we recognized we would have to engage in what has become known in the entrepreneur ranks as "bootstrapping." As the term implies, we'd have to pull ourselves up by our own bootstraps which would include re-investing any income back into the company. Translation? The Bank of Andrea and Allen Beach would be funding this venture.

Bootstrapping your business means you do not rely on external sources like venture capitalists or angel investors for funding. Instead, you start your business on whatever cash and credit you can personally raise. It means thinking in opposite terms of what you might want to: instead of figuring out how much money you need (or want), you focus on how to make it work with how much you already have.

Working with the little you have rather than the lot you'd like to have is the situation for nearly everyone opening a business. Don't let yourself become disheartened over everything you don't have or can't get quickly enough. Instead, focus on how far you can stretch what you do have and how far it can get you. What you may currently see as a deficiency may actually be a blessing in disguise. There are a number of advantages to bootstrapping a company and being forced to work with a very small amount of start-up capital is actually one of them. There's nothing like being cash-strapped to make you work extremely hard for a sale! You'll be putting in a lot of sweat equity to begin with, but if you focus your efforts in the right areas, this is 100% to your advantage. There's no greater learning experience than plunging right in and doing it yourself. We consider ourselves extremely fortunate to have built both companies from the ground up. We have literally worked all the jobs required to keep Argus Rising running, so although these days we concentrate on executive duties and delegate much of the rest, we know each facet of the business backward and forward and can jump in anywhere if that's what's required.

Bootstrapping, let us add, is by no means relegated to small businesses. Can a bootstrapped start-up become a large company? You bet it can. Ever heard of Dell? Microsoft? eBay? They were all bootstrapped initially.

Actually, there's evidence to suggest that bootstrapped companies are more likely to succeed than ones backed by venture capitalists or other outside investors. We only have to point to the dot-com bust as hundreds if not thousands of start-up companies that were well financed bit the dust with little to nothing to show for it. Instead of focusing on producing a good product and generating revenue, they seemed to be focused on how they could spend all the investment dollars they had.

They in fact had lots of investment capital and that may have been their undoing. Don't think there's such a thing as being over-financed? Think again! Having scads of money at your disposal before you've started generating sales can cause you to focus on building infrastructure instead of building a functioning business that actually sells something and makes a profit. Remember, nothing happens until you sell something.

Yet another advantage to bootstrapping your company is that you won't have a third party involved in your affairs. There are plenty of relationships between venture capitalists and entrepreneurs that are completely amicable, but there are an equal number of cautionary tales (if not outright horror stories) of start-ups who underestimated the ever-vigilant eye of Big Brother. Whatever the relationship with investors, you're accountable to them and you'll have the added pressure of making money for them. And you'd better believe that they'll pull the plug if you don't bring in the dollars! Some people flower under this kind of pressure; some people wilt. We hope you're of the former type if you're going to make it as an entrepreneur, but either way, if you don't like the idea of outsiders being involved in your business, bootstrapping is for you. In our case, we chose not to go the venture-capitalist route because we wanted to be beholden to no one but ourselves, and more importantly, we had formulated a solid plan to raise start-up capital. (And remember, part of that plan was having a contingency plan in case any worst-case scenarios occurred.)

So, where do you go to get money if you're going to strike out as a lone miner and find the money on your own? There are entire books written on this subject and we will not try to cover every detail of every option, so we recommend that you select one of the better books and put in some research hours beyond this chapter. A few we relied on back in the 90s were *Winning Strategies for Capital Formation* by Linda Chandler and *Financing Your Business Dreams with Other People's Money* by Harold R. Lacy, and there are several very good ones that have been published more recently, including *How to Raise All the Money You Need for Any Business* by Tyler G. Hicks and *Go Big or Go Home* by Will Schroter. We wish we could tell you that our hunt for start-up capital went off without a hitch, but the fact of the matter is we would change several things. This is actually good news for you, as you have the opportunity to learn from our mistakes. As we all know, hindsight is always 20/20.

Let's start with a list of possible options; we'll cover the positive and negatives of each. This list is not all-inclusive but it is a good list of the most realistic options for a first-time entrepreneur, especially in tough economic times. We have personally used four of these options: we used numbers 1, 2 to obtain our initial start-up cash, and once we established our business we supplemented with 4 and 5. We'll list them in descending order of most realistic sources to least. Obviously, there is an infinite number of possibilities, but these are the major sources of capital and will assist you in understanding where to spend your time.

List for Start-up Capital Sources:

1. Your personal cash
2. Credit cards
3. Crowdfunding [there are many to choose from]
4. Employee partnerships
5. Business loans
6. Venture capitalist / Angel investors

1. **Your personal cash** – Your personal assets are the simplest and surest way to raise start-up capital. How much money do you have set aside, how much do you have in retirement accounts that you can tap, and what are you willing to risk? We were ready to risk everything with the knowledge that we had the skills to start from zero and rebuild if we had to. Between savings and tapping into our 401(k)s we raised $8,000 in personal cash.

- Advantages – Easy to access. It's all yours and you won't owe anybody a dime
- Disadvantage – It's all yours and will be gone once you use it

2. **Credit cards** – Once again this is a very simple way to raise capital for a start-up, which is one of the reasons that personal credit cards are one of the most frequent sources of money for a bootstrapped company.

- Advantage – Easy to access
- Disadvantage – You are limited on what you can use the money for and you're looking at expensive financing

3. **Crowdfunding -**

- Indiegogo - Originally launched with a focus on film, Indiegogo pivoted to include funding for literally anything and is becoming known for financing personal and cause-related campaigns such as that for the bullied bus monitor, which raised over $700,000. It accepts all projects without review. As Indiegogo says on its website, "Our platform is available to anyone, anywhere, to raise money for anything." While its success fee at 4 percent is 1 percent lower than most websites (which charge 5 percent), it does charge one of the highest fees in the industry -- 9 percent -- if you don't meet your goal.

- Kickstarter - The most well-known of the crowdfunding websites, Kickstarter focuses on creative endeavors including design, the arts (film, publishing, music), gaming and technology. While Kickstarter can't be used to fund businesses per se, it does accept products and has had some remarkably successful campaigns, including about 50 that have generated over a million dollars in funding.

4.   **Employee Partnerships** – You can entice key employees to join the company with little to no pay for a set period of time in exchange for partial ownership. We did not leverage this option but with hindsight, we should have.   Because we both grew up in the technology world and neither one of us really had the skills to be a CFO, we hired outside CPAs and financial consultants to assist us with making sound financial

decisions. This was truly a mistake. Outside assistance has no skin in the game and when it comes down to it they could care less if you survive or die. If we had it to do over we would have found an experienced start-up CFO who wanted ownership in a young start-up company and was willing to gain stock through sweat equity instead of a large paycheck.

- Advantage – You can gain some real talent to help you grow the business without dipping into your start-up capital
- Disadvantage – You give up equity in the business. Be very careful how much you give up between this and equity financing

5. **Business loans (Bank / Small Business Association (SBA) loans)** – This one is straightforward but be ready to sign a personal responsibility clause that attaches your personal assets. We did not qualify for any bank loan until we had a solid Accounts Receivable and, even then, we had to sign a personal responsibility clause. Over the life of our company, we went from not qualifying for a loan to having a $250,000 line of credit and a $150,000 SBA loan and then back to zero during the recession of 2008-09.

- Advantage – Flexible line of credit that can be drawn on for immediate cash needs
- Disadvantage – The bank gets into your business and can recall the loan at any time for any reason. They also require monthly reports on the status of your financials. The application process and ongoing reports can be invasive and time-consuming

6.   **Venture Capitalist / Angel Investors** – An outside source provides you with capital in return for a percentage of your profits. Both venture capitalists and angel investors tend to look for large deals or already-established companies.

- Advantage – You can potentially raise lots of start-up capital without acquiring debt. VCs and AIs often will lead you to business that you would not have gotten without their contacts
- Disadvantage – The process of finding a Venture Capitalist or an Angel Investor is very time-consuming and the odds of getting financed are close to zero. If you do get financed, expect your investors to be in your business on a monthly basis. They will own equity in your company. They are generally invasive and if they have enough equity, they can and will fire you if they believe it is in the best interest of the company

You can find endless advice on this subject on the Internet but we suspect you will find yourself in a never-ending research loop looking at fringe options that simply are not realistic for the average first-time entrepreneur. Unless you have an unusual situation that allows you to obtain cash from a different source, our strong recommendation is to stick to the Top 5 and the books that we've recommended.

Next, let's look at some basic questions to consider regarding the cash you need:

1. Is the cash a long-term or a short-term requirement?

2. Will you use it for daily operating expenses or capital purchases such as equipment or a building?

3. Is this an immediate need or can you spread out the requirement over weeks or even months?

4. What options are you comfortable with?

Once you've got your answers, now what? Now you need to predict the future. Meaning, you need to estimate business volume and predict the cash needed to support that volume with a buffer built in. Nothing mysterious here, this takes into account all fixed costs, expected sales, the cost of filling sales along with expected time frames that we would get paid for the sales, and predicts a cash investment needed to support the start-up.

Let's say you raised $8,000 of your own cash and want to start a Drone Photography business. Let's sweeten the scenario and also say that you've come up with a way to do it differently than all of the others, you have a culture you want to build, photography has been a hobby for years but this is your first business. Let's look at how the numbers break down. (*Please note that these are not realistic figures*. We simply want to provide an example of what you need to do prior to launching your Drone business to figure out how much investment capital you need and how to manage it to your advantage.)

Bottom-Line Necessities to Start:

- Drone & 4K Camera - $2,940.00
- Miscellaneous assets, Website, FAA Remote Pilot License, Drone Training, etc. - $1,400
- Buffer – 10% of total expenses - $440
- Salary - $75,000 per month; you should be able to go the first 120 days with no salary
- Miscellaneous Monthly Expenses - $2,000
- **Total startup expense - $4,774.00 Cash + $2,000 per month not including future salary**

Sales Data:

- Average sales per event - $1,800
- Do the math: Once your salary kicks-in you need to be booking at least 5 events per month just to break even. So, how long will it take you to ramp up to 5 events per month and what does the ramp look like?
- Forecast month #1 – 0 events
- Forecast month #2 – 3 events
- Forecast month #3 – 5 events

These numbers are minus the initial investment dollars:
- Month #1 expense = $2,000 / Revenue = $0 – Delta = negative $2,000
- Month #2 expense = $2,000 / Revenue = $5,400 – Profit = + $1,400
- Month #3 expense = $2,000 / Revenue = $9,000 – Profit = + $8,400

Good job! You've made your first profit, but guess what? If you're paying attention, you'll also realize that you personally have not made a penny, so now get back to work. Don't be disheartened; patience and persistence will pay off.

At the end of the day it's up to you to find the means to launch your business—no one is going to be standing around on the sidelines with a signed blank check. Entrepreneurs are proficient at mining every possible gold nugget and using each to their best advantage. They're natural bootstrappers! So, let the mining begin!

CHAPTER SIX NOTES:
The Hunt for Start-up Capital –
How Much and Where to Get It

- For the average first-time entrepreneur, start-up capital will be meager and hard to come by, even in the best of economies. But view this as an opportunity. Strategize shrewdly: make the most of what you do have and let the hunger for profit drive you to sell, sell, sell.
- Venture capitalists and angel investors can be excellent sources of start-up capital, and if this is what's right for you and your business, by all means leverage this option.
- Don't underestimate the power of bootstrapping. Hunting for and acquiring your own start-up funds is a valuable learning experience and prevents you from having to answer to outside investors.
- Start-up capital resources are as follows:
  1. Personal Cash
  2. Credit Cards
  3. Crowdfunding
  4. Employee Partnerships
  5. Business Loans
  6. Venture Capitalists / Angel Investors
- Use every bit of your resourcefulness and creativity to find the start-up capital you need to get your business off the ground, and then turn all your efforts to making that first sale.

CHAPTER SEVEN
Sales, The Miners Most Important Pursuit
Finding your First Gold Nugget

Grab your highlighter and get ready to learn: this may be the single most important chapter in the book. If you read nothing else, make sure you read and understand this chapter! It won't teach you how to sell, but it will explain what we consider to be the foundational principle for successful sales in any economy, any market. It's called the Sales Equation, and it looks like this:

Relationship + Solution + Price = a Sale
It is so simple it's astonishing!
The basic elements never change

What does change is the *percentage of importance* of each element. The percentages will change depending on what type of business you're in. For Argus Rising, the *relationship* factor has the highest percentage. The Argus' Sales Equation looks like this:

Relationship @ 70% + Solution @ 25% + Price @ 5% = a Sale

In other words, 70% of our sale is the relationship we build with the clients during training; 25% is the solution we provide which, in this case, is not only unique it was co-developed by First Responders, and 5% is left for the price.

Let's examine this equation, factor by factor. It is important that you determine the correct Sales Equation variables for *your* business, as the percentages are different for every business, and it's also important to realize that you *can* change the Sales Equation, as we'll show you below. Let us explain the equation by showing you how it works at Argus Rising.

Relationship

Let's say we have the right Solution and the right Price. Sounds good, doesn't it? Maybe even like a sure deal. But for Argus Rising this means we only have 30% of the sale completed. Without the right relationship we will *not* close the deal.

This is a difficult concept for many people to accept because it disrupts our notion of what's considered fair. In most people's minds, "fair" means that the right Solution at the right Price will win every time. At first glance this assessment seems accurate, but guess what? This is rarely how the world actually works. (And trust us: if you're counting on the world to be fair, do not become an entrepreneur or you will be very disappointed.) Unless you have something really unique, something that everyone wants, you have to turn loose of this notion of what's fair and what isn't or you will not succeed.

Solution and price are certainly important, but in our model, it's *relationship* that rules the day. People do business with people they know and trust. It's just that simple!

Let's say we have the relationship with a client but we don't have the solution and the right price. Not to worry! We can still make the sale because the relationship we have with the decision makers is the primary factor in closing the deal. For proof, simply look at our first training course, we literally had no first responder course and did not know what to charge but we had the relationship (70% of the deal) and they trusted us to develop a course tailored to their specific requirements. If we have the relationship, the client will give us the feedback and the time we need to develop the right solution at the right price. Thus, the relationship for us is 70% of the sale. People do business with people they know and trust.

Here's just one story that illustrates how our *relationship* with the decision makers is vital in making a sale. Allen had a well-established relationship with a Fire Chief (we'll call him Brad) of a large Fire Department. Because Brad was well acquainted with Allen and his principles, he knew that if Allen made a commitment it was more than just a company commitment—it was also a *personal* commitment to complete the work on time, to stay on budget, and to ensure the client's satisfaction.

So, when Brad needed to train his team on Drones over a two-week period, one of the companies he turned to was Argus Rising, even though Argus was at that time both the smallest and the youngest of the companies competing for the bid. It was critical that this go smoothly and it was mandatory for his team to pass the FAA Remote Pilot Test and be capable of flying actual missions. A large competitor was bidding the entire training project including providing customized Drones. By this time Argus had completed numerous first responder training classes, but we had never provided customized Drones as part of the deal and we had zero experience in pricing such a large project. We told Brad we'd love to help but that we'd bid only on the training portion. Our offer, however, did not work for Brad—he wanted a single, streamlined solution. "Sorry, guys," he said. "It's all or nothing."

We wanted the business, and we knew Brad wanted us to have the business. So, we scheduled several planning sessions with Brad, and in the end, we assembled the right solution at the appropriate price and won the bid. Those planning sessions were crucial to our winning the contract, and they wouldn't have been possible without a strong relationship. *Relationship* was without a doubt the primary factor in making this sale.

On the flip side, we've lost deals in which we had a unique solution and an excellent price but didn't have the relationship. What happened? The decision maker took our solution and gave it to our competitor who did have the relationship and awarded them the business. That is the power of a relationship.

Is that "fair"? Fair or not, it's the reality of sales.

Remember that the relationship sword cuts both ways and you just have to gut it up and get on with it. This scenario underscores how very important the *relationship* part of the Sales Equation is—it can garner big wins if you have it or cost you big losses if you don't.

The successful entrepreneur, however, learns a lesson from every sale lost (and by doing so, steadily increases his or her win-to-loss ratio). This is as good a time as any to discuss the proper way to exit when you lose business. Regardless of the reason you lost it, it's absolutely critical that you provide your client a professional exit. Sales is all about the long haul. Never burn a bridge because you feel wronged— unprofessional exits will always come back to haunt you. Take your lumps without complaint (without any public complaining anyway), and let it inspire you to find new ways to build relationships and expand your business. Through patience and persistence, you can win that client back. *Relationship* prevails and preserves connections.

Before we move on to the *solutions* part of the Sales Equation, let us put a potential fear to rest. Some of you may be feeling that relying so heavily on relationship is not an appropriate way for a business to conduct itself. But let us assure you that there's absolutely nothing wrong with doing business with people you know and trust, and here's why.

Imagine that you have a particular need to fill and three companies show you their products and solutions. They all meet your company's needs, and they're all priced within 20% of each other. What do you do? The wisest decision is to go with the people you know and trust. Why?

1. You know they will deliver the product as they said they would
2. You know that they will fix any problems that arise
3. You know they will stick to their quoted price

All of these factors have at least a 20% value in your decision-making process. It pays to do business with people you know and trust.

There are no business ethical issues with relying heavily on relationship to do business—the decision makers are simply watching out for the welfare of their company. And, remember that no client is going to make a business-buy decision based purely on relationship without regard to solution and price. We have never closed a deal on relationship alone.

Solution

This is your service / curriculum / product / presentation / format / design / or any other factors that make up your offering and how you present it to your potential clients. It is in the solution that you can gain competitive advantages. In trying to do so, always remember to *do something, anything, differently.* We are very fortunate in that we are able to bring unique and exceptionally valuable training solutions to the table for our First Responders. As we are a service company, our solutions always start with our people. As you've seen, we believe that if you take care of your frontline people they will take care of your clients, and that philosophy has consistently worked well for us.

Our competitive advantage, however, extends well beyond our people, and it has to be redefined in every deal that we sell. We frequently compete with other large companies, and while that may seem like a disadvantage, it's actually our strength. Large companies have well-defined solutions, and they're constantly trying to sell those solutions. Frequently, however, those solutions don't fit with the client's needs—the larger the company the less flexibility they have in changing their solutions. This is exactly where smaller businesses can gain the competitive advantage. Our size makes us more flexible and more nimble; in many cases, we can act more quickly. We listen to clients' specific needs and work to understand their particular problems. Then we present a solution that's highly specific to that client's needs. When we combine a winning solution with the right relationship and the right price, we win every time.

Price

There are many companies that lead their sales campaigns with price. In an industry in which you sell a commodity and you can gain economies of scale through volume business, then leading with price may work. For our purposes, "economies of scale" refers to the notion of increasing profit percentages as the volume of sales increases. Good examples are Southwest Airlines and Wal-Mart, who offer bargain prices but are profitable through sheer volume of sales. Wal-Mart's model is a simple one of leveraging their volume-purchasing to reduce their cost and thus increase their profit percentage while delivering low cost to consumers. Southwest Airlines gains economies of scale by filling as many seats as possible. The relative cost of flying a plane from Dallas to Los Angeles does not change; what does change is the number of tickets sold. Southwest's profit percentage increases significantly if they can fill all the seats on a flight, and they do that by offering low fares to consumers. These are two excellent models of being able to significantly increase profit percentages while competing primarily on a price basis.

Please note that we are discussing profit *percentages*. Do not confuse this with increased profits. You must have more than increased profits to survive in a commodity-based sales world. For example, if you sell five widgets at $100 each and your profit is $20 per widget (20%), then your profit for the five widgets is $100. If you increase your volume of sales to ten widgets, your profit increases to $200 but you haven't changed your profit percentage—it's still 20%. This increase in volume has produced more profit dollars but it has not produced an increase in profit percentage, therefore there are no "economies of scale" from the increased sales.

In our business, leading with price is a sure way to go out of business. Time after time, we've watched our competitors do just that. In businesses like ours that do not sell a commodity, we do have some economies of scale and if we can change the conversation from price to # of attendees we all win. Then why do our competitors lead with price? It's because they're making the mistake of confusing *revenue* with *profit*. It's a deadly mistake for a young company to make.

Knowing the difference between revenue and profit sounds like a Business 101 concept, but you'd be surprised at how many people can get swept up in a large deal and forget to look at the profit. Especially if you're just starting out, high-value deals can have a way of distracting you from making sound business decisions, and the higher the value the more the confusion. You think, *Wow, $100,000! If we can win this we'll be on our way!* Well, not really.

You have to know two things:

- First, you must know the *true* profit-value of that dreamy-sounding $100,000. Total up all your costs and throw in an extra 10% for good measure, and then see what you have left over—

there's how much your $100K is worth. (And by the way, don't lie to yourself about costs. People do this all the time and lying to yourself is a sure path back to corporate America.)

- Second, you must know the lowest price you can accept for the deal. It can't be $100,000 or you have no room for negotiation. Don't make the mistake of thinking that you can overcome a zero-profit deal by making it up in volume. No way! No matter how many products you sell, zero is still zero. If there was ever a time to put your ego on the shelf, this is it. Your ego will kill for this deal—in fact your ego is already planning a trip to the local hang-out tonight and figuring out a way to casually announce, "I closed a $100,000 deal today!" Your ego hasn't the slightest concern for profit or your long-term success, so tell your ego to stay home. Train your ego to want to say, "I closed a deal today at 40% gross profit." Sure, it doesn't sound as sexy, but like avoiding that piece of chocolate cake after dinner, it will pay off in the long run.

And if your ego still protests? Okay, give it a *small* piece of chocolate cake tonight, but never forget that a zero-profit deal is worse than no deal at all because it takes your time and attention away from closing good deals, the ones you need to create long-term success.

Okay, so how do you determine the percentage value of price in your Sales Equation? You have to decide if what you are selling is going to be a commodity. (And yes, you actually do get to make that decision.) What is a commodity? It is a physical good that is bought and sold based solely on its price, rather than quality and features. It is getting where many of today's consumers consider a Drone a commodity. A Drone is a Drone, and as long as it's from one of the primary manufacturers, then all that matters is price and thus it is a commodity.

Let's say that your service or product is a commodity and in order to reduce overhead and investment you're going to use Amazon to move it. In that case you'll need to lead with price and your equation could be:

$$\text{Price @ 70\%} + \text{Solution @ 25\%}$$
$$+ \text{Relationship @ 5\%} = \text{a Sale}$$

If this is your business model for Drone sales, then clearly you have to find economies of scale through a volume business, or else you can count on having a short-term company. Why? Because with this model, you'll never have enough profit to build a competitive advantage and invest in the future. Without these things, you won't survive long-term. This is a huge reason so many start-ups go out of business within the first few years. They can never make enough of a profit to spend toward staying ahead of the competition and/or preparing for the future. They're too busy struggling to pay today's bills to think about long-range planning.

Now, what happens if what you've chosen is a commodity and you can't find a way to gain economies of scale? The time has come to ask yourself if you can turn a commodity into a non-commodity so that you don't have to lead with price.

Most business classes will teach you the answer is No, a commodity is a commodity but in reality, the answer is Yes!

To prove this theory let's take a look at a success story of turning a commodity into a non-commodity. There's no better place to look than Starbucks. Coffee is one of the world's standard commodities. Yet Starbucks transformed coffee into one of the most successful non-commodities in recent memory and captured the lion's share of the coffee-drinking market. Starbucks had two choices when they built their business model:

1) treat coffee as a commodity and fight for market share based on price or

2) turn it into a non-commodity, increase the price by two and three times the current market price and hope for the best. Starbucks chose the non-commodity route and is now the world's largest coffeehouse chain.

How did they do it? They did something no coffee company had ever done before. They did something differently.

They branded a look and a feel. This has less to do with the actual product, the coffee, and far more to do with the ambience of a coffee house and how it makes consumers feel. Certainly, Starbucks serves great drinks (We swear by their hot chocolate, and Dark Roast flows through Andrea's veins), but when it comes down to it, their success is all about the coffee house experience. They've captured—and replicated in every Starbucks shop all over the world—the ambience of the traditional European café. They created an empire by convincing consumers that drinking specialty coffee in a comfortable, inviting environment is worth the price of a cup. The "Starbucks Experience" is an elusive model that competitors try to duplicate, but none have succeeded in toppling Starbucks.

So, do you want to lead your sale with price, or focus on doing *something, anything, differently?* The answer can be found by taking a look at the Starbucks Sales Equation:

$$\text{Relationship @ } 70\% + \text{Solution @ } 25\% + \text{Price @ } 5\% = \text{a Sale}$$

Hmm, that looks familiar! Starbucks builds a relationship with their clients through their unique coffee house environment *first* (relationship), they deliver an excellent cup of coffee *second* (solution), and then price becomes almost a moot point.

The Bottom Line
Now that you're fully acquainted with each part of the Sales Equation, what do you think yours will be? Record your Sales Equation here:

Relationship @ _____ %
** + Solution @ _____ %**
**   + Price @ _____ % = a Sale**

Make no bones about it: NOTHING HAPPENS IN THE WORLD OF BUSINESS UNTIL YOU **SELL** SOMETHING. You can have the most talented people, the most well-developed business plan, and all the energy and creativity in the world, but *profitable sales* are the driving force behind a successful company. No matter what industry you're in, you will not stay in business for long without understanding how to make sales profitable.

The Sales Equation is an excellent tool for knowing how to make profitable sales for your particular business. The percentage of importance for each element will vary from business to business, but if you determine the correct percentages for your company and formulate your sales strategy accordingly, you'll win every time.

Chapter Seven Notes:
Sales, The Miners Most Important Pursuit
Finding your First Gold Nugget

- Nothing happens until you sell something. Allow me to repeat, NOTHING HAPPENS UNTIL YOU SELL SOMETHING!
- The foundational principle for successful sales is the Sales Equation. Its basic elements do not change:

Relationship + Solution + Price = a Sale

- Understanding your ideal Sales Equation is key to formulating your sales strategy and maintaining your long-term success.
- The relationship variable concerns your connection with the decision makers. Cultivate strong ties with potential and current clients. Relationship can win deals you'd otherwise lose.
- To gain the competitive advantage with your solution, do *something, anything, differently.* Create a unique way to fill a client's need.
- If you don't like your current Sales Equation, look for ways to change it.
- It is possible to change a commodity to a non-commodity. Study companies who have done so successfully and emulate their success.

CHAPTER EIGHT
The Trailblazers
Drone Start-Up Success Stories

Let's switch tracks for a moment and talk to some of the "Trailblazers' who have started their own Drone Business and have found success in this unique fast paced industry.

Richard Gill. Richard is the President and Founder of Drone Defence providing Anti-Drone Systems and Services www.dronedefence.co.uk. Drone Defence is the UK's first drone focused security consultancy.

Debin Ray. Debin is the Co-Founder and Managing Director of Desert Rotor. Debin and team design and supply Ground Control Systems for global leaders in Unmanned Vehicles www.desertrotor.com.

Bob Schmidt. Bob is the President and Founder of UAV Propulsion Tech, a US based company that markets advanced UAV technology from global entities into the United States' Unmanned Aerial Vehicle market. www.uavpropulsiontech.com

Richard Gill, President and Founder
Drone Defence www.Dronedefence.co.uk

Richard Gill is the founder and CEO of Drone Defence, Richard has an MBA along with extensive military and executive leadership skills. Drone Defence is the UK's first drone focused security consultancy offering the latest technology, techniques, and procedures to help organizations protect themselves from the harmful use of commercial drone technology. Drone Defence won the FSB East Midlands, "Start-Up Business" of the Year Award. Richard believes that drone technology will change the way we view, interact with and move around the world. Like all transformative technologies Unmanned Aerial Vehicles will have a tremendous impact on the way we live our lives.

Can you briefly walk us through your story; how you started and how you got to where you are today?

I spent 10 years in the British Army being a logistics officer so on a day-to-day basis, I was moving things around and looking after people and, then, also deploying to Iraq & Afghanistan. It was in Afghanistan in 2012 when my interest in Drones first started. I was serving with the 20th Armored Brigade in Helmand Province in Southern Afghanistan in the Brigade Headquarters in Lashkargah and I saw how Drones of all shapes and sizes were being used by Coalition Forces to gather really vital and life-saving information on certain activity. I observed big Drones in the sky monitoring large areas to smaller Drones looking out for IED's / roadside bombs to really tiny ones that soldiers carried around in their pockets to put into compounds and over walls to see if there were any threats or dangers on the other side. I saw how putting a sensor on a small flying object to go and check something out first could really have huge commercial benefits in the civilian world. When I considered people inspecting roofs and putting themselves in harm's way to get information, I thought Drones could be used to gather information and make things safer for lots of different industries. These observations are what got me interested in the Drone industry.

In 2014 I left the Army and started out in my first venture which was a Drone surveying and mapping business with a business partner. While I was going through the process of trying to generate sales for mapping and surveying videography, I was repeatedly asked about how Drones had been used to fly in Iraq and even how they had been flown illegally, such as flying drugs into prisons That got me thinking about how I could use my previous security knowledge and couple that with my new-found Drone knowledge to produce a solution to combat the irresponsible and illegal use of Drones. I think it's worth mentioning at this point, that I got into the Drone industry because I could see huge potential. I could see that Drones were changing the way we view and interact with the world and that eventually this change would move completely around the planet. What I'm trying to do is everything I can to demonstrate the potential of Drones and prevent their misuse while acting as a really critical commercial enabler. We're at the start of a brand new industry and it's great to be here.

What are some of the barriers you have had to overcome along the way?

The barriers have been numerous, to be honest. Trying to sell a concept and a product into a brand new market that did not exist previously is difficult. If you look at any business studies book, they would recommend that you bring a new product into an established market or create a new market within an established product. With the Drone industry it was a new product – new industry – typically not something you'd look at to be successful early on. Here we were at the very beginning of this industry

From my personal point of view the barriers I had to work with were getting financing for a small business, getting it off the ground and trying to make sales and satisfying customer's expectations in a brand new industry. However, I think that the business case for Drone use is developing at a rapid pace; more money is currently being spent in the Drone industry in the UK and worldwide.

So, what inspired you to fly a Drone across the English Channel? What challenges did you have to overcome?

What inspired me to do the flight across the English Channel was more of a challenge in numerous ways. It was challenge of doing it for myself and my company; it was to better understand the technology and its limitations and then almost as a marketing exercise. To demonstrate that we are successful in what we do and this is what the technology can do would validate our industry recognition and experience. The main driver to do it was to show that we are successfully pushing the boundaries of Drone technology.

In February 2016 – Drone technology was still pretty new and advancing at a phenomenal rate so everything I used to build that Drone was absolutely cutting edge, batteries formed a large portion of the Drone's upper weight. We were using massive propellers and big motors to generate the required lift to give it the endurance we needed to fly across the Channel.

One of the main limitations was the fact that, according to the rules, we were not allowed to fly autonomously. We had to stay within visual line of sight of within 500 meters. To maintain visual line of sight, I had to be in an aircraft flying the Drone or in a boat in the water following it across the channel. At that time there weren't many boats that could keep up with the Drone, so that was a limiting factor to the Drone's performance relating to how quickly we could cross the Channel. I eventually found a boat that could do 30 knots and that meant the Drone could fly across the Channel in about 75 minutes. Given the batteries and the construction of the platform I had developed; 75 minutes was about 80% of the Drone's endurance capability. So, I knew we could do it. I built two Drones just in case one crashed which it inevitably did. Every other flight ended in total disaster, failure, and the complete destruction of a Drone. I spent a lot of time building, refining and changing the position of the batteries to give it a better center of gravity. Two days before the scheduled attempt in February 2016, my backup Drone crashed on the final test flight and I was down to one Drone. I couldn't carry out anymore testing so I just had to go with that single Drone.

Thankfully, everything came together and my team and I flew across the Channel! The time was 72 minutes and I believe at the time it was the longest single flight of a Drone and quite certainly it was the first crossing of the English Channel with a quadcopter. And, yes! We set some records doing that.

Let's talk business! Tell us about your company; what should we know?

Drone Defense is all about preventing the misuse of commercial Drone technology that we see in the press, not only in the UK, but worldwide. There's lots of negative press coverage on how Drones are being misused and I think the response to that is that legislators and then governments come under pressure to regulate the use of Drones. So we've seen this in the UK, we've seen it in the US as well, where Drones of all shapes and sizes have to be registered and I think it's a very negative step. I believe that the more access people have to the technology the quicker it will be accepted. Innovators, entrepreneurs and really clever people will figure out ways of making money out of Drone technology so any barrier to accessing the technology is a negative one. Drone Defense's sole purpose is to provide a viable and economic solution to prevent people from misusing technology.

How do we do that? Well, we focus on a number of key markets and use electronic counter measures to essentially disrupt the Drone's ability to fly in restricted air space. So, I have a number of products including a portable system called Dynopis E1000 that is designed to give temporary protection. A more permanent system, SkyFence, is designed to basically create an electronic barrier that Drones cannot fly through, such as prisons and airports where you wouldn't want any Drones at anytime.

We are currently working on a new project called Omniscient – the purpose of Omniscient is to monitor all Drone usage over a wide area and use that information to allow Drones to fly collaboratively with each other and to integrate them into other airspace, monitor aviation, and provide situation awareness to people who have a legitimate concern about Drones going or flying near their buildings. Things are really progressing well and we should hopefully have something worth shouting about soon.

Any shout-outs? Who else deserves credit in this story?

Certainly, family and friends have supported me through this entire journey. Life was reasonably comfortable in the Army and leaving was by far the hardest thing I've ever done. The lack of financial security and committing myself to the fight to succeed has been enormously stressful, not only on me, but the whole family.

Finally, any advice you can share for the new Drone entrepreneur?

In the UK we have this thing call a Phantom Millionaire. We've essentially had an explosion the last three years from a few hundred commercial Drone operators to I think over 5,000 operators today. People have gone out and bought the DJI Phantom and thought - Now I'm going to take pictures of real estate and take videos for TV and make a lot of money. Sadly, a lot of those people go out of business in the first 12 months, there is a lot more to this than purchasing a drone and building a web-site.

My advice to Drone entrepreneurs is to *Really Carve a Niche and Add Value.* People must take a look at their personal skills, their network and how they are going to enhance offerings within their area of influence using Drone technology. Potentially if you were already a surveyor or a building engineer, or something like that, adopting a new technology and bringing a new product into the established market is the way to go – **be aggressive, be utterly aggressive and focused on adding value.** I think a lot of people see the technology, get qualifications, set up a website, and then expect business to roll in. Anyone who has run a small business for any length of time will realize that being able to deliver services is reasonably straightforward once you've got the skills and expertise. Finding and satisfying a customer is by far the most difficult thing. People really need to focus on marketing, going out there selling and making a name for themselves, and becoming known in the industry to positively influence the conversation.

Debin Ray, Co-Founder and Managing Director Desert Rotor www.desertrotor.com

Debin Ray is the Co-Founder and Managing Director of Desert Rotor. Debin has a MBA along with extensive UAV and leadership experience. Debin and team designed and now supply Ground Control Systems for global leaders in UAV design.

Can you briefly walk us through your story; how you started and how you got to where you are today.

The Desert Rotor startup story is a fascinating mix of fortunate experiences, chance meetings and a drive to make an impact in a blossoming industry. *It started with passion.* Before the Desert Rotor team formally came together we all shared a passion that naturally brought us together. The passion was flying aggressive, loud and extremely fast 3D aerobatic R/C airplanes. By chance we met each other at the Sun Valley Fliers Club in Cave Creek, Arizona. For many years we enjoyed flying R/C airplanes as a hobby and spent countless hours bonding with the R/C community.

One day I overheard one of our friends talking about multirotor Drones and that one would soon be released with a GoPro camera. I looked into this further and realized a lot of the components being used in Drones were the same used in the R/C world. The commercial Drone industry was pulling from R/C technology and this was very exciting for me. I pre-ordered, many months in advance, a quadcopter that could hold a GoPro camera and had a GPS enabled autopilot system.

I was going through a very challenging time in my personal life at that time. I had an infant daughter and was going through a very traumatic divorce. I was working at a large global financial services company and hitting rock bottom professionally as well. I had worked at the company for around 10 years only to realize I wasn't passionate about my role and career progression. For many years I was haunted with the fact I was meant for something else and didn't know what that was. I knew I had to be smart about it and still perform great at my job, earn money and slowly invest into things I was passionate about. Not making any rash decisions was very key.

As my personal life crashed dramatically, I felt I needed to focus on positive things that I was passionate about. I felt this would naturally help me rebuild a happy life and be a good father. Luckily for me around this exact moment, my quadcopter arrived. I unboxed it and right then I knew instantly I had to start a company and at least present myself as someone who knew about Drones.

I used income from my financial services job to get some logos designed, a website domain and parts for my Drone fleet that I was building. I spent thousands of hours learning, building and figuring out every aspect of a Drone. Initially I didn't know what Desert Rotor was or would do. I thought if I became a Drone expert something would take shape. This proved to be the case.

Only a few months after starting Desert Rotor in 2014, some professionals at a major defense company in Arizona heard about my company through the flying club. I knew immediately I needed the right partners to be with me in these first initial meetings. I reached out to two friends who happen to be brilliant engineers in their professional lives. I would have never known them if I wasn't a member at the Sun Valley Fliers R/C club. Having a deep solid network will always pay off in the long-term.

It is key to lineup with those who share the same passions and have a natural motivation to want to achieve big things. Offering partnership and ownership in Desert Rotor helped with the motivation towards that vision. We attended various meetings at this defense company to discuss their requirements on a large project they were doing with unmanned ground vehicles. They were also probing if we were a solid team that could help them lift their R&D substantially. We won a two-part contract to help them with their unmanned efforts which included designing controllers to operate unmanned technology vast distances away. We had the basic knowledge and knew theoretically we could achieve their requirements. After long nights and weekends, we were able to not only fulfill their technology requirements, we exceeded them in a number of ways. We continue to have a close client relationship with this defense company.

Around late 2014 we decided we needed a signature product to establish Desert Rotor for the long-term. We were fortunate to earn good money from our defense work and allocated about 95% of it towards developing our signature product. The three of us held salaried jobs as our primary source of income. This was key as we were able to bootstrap Desert Rotor. "Bootstrapping" is when you take revenues from existing client work to build the company instead of outside investments. This has allowed us to maintain complete control over Desert Rotor to this day. I personally would put 100% of my bonuses and large chunks of my salary from my day job towards Desert Rotor. I knew it was crucial for the team to not have insane deadlines and pressure during the product development phases. We decided we wanted to design a ground control system [GCS] with fully integrated flight controls that could interface with any aircraft type and most RF based autopilot systems. This was a high bar at the time, so we tried to achieve all that in stages through designing various prototypes. Every prototype we made was a success, so we just kept throwing more requirements at it. We had zero sales, investor or financial pressure during this process. I didn't want Desert Rotor to be another startup with overhyped vaporware and under deliver. From 2014 to 2017 we designed 5 generations of ground control systems in-house. The 5th one was the one we decided to sell commercially in September 2017. We did market the platform for a year leading up to the 5th generation. We timed it where we gave all the leads we had a no-pressure sales approach. When we were ready to produce & sell, we lowered the price and offered a new version that had much more functionality. It became an instant no-brainer to our clients. We immediately established a large group of clients using this strategy.

Our systems are now piloting and operating commercial Drones 24 hours a day, 7 days a week. Our clients are global leaders in unmanned aircraft design and use Desert Rotor exclusively as their GCS supplier.

There was a lot of sacrifice, three years of development and sizable investments across the board before we even allowed our product on the market. Minimizing the sales pressure initially, allowing appropriate product development timeframes and not allowing outside investors to dictate the pace of our business helped us build success on our own terms.

The company is growing quickly and we have all resigned our previous positions to focus all our efforts towards being the GCS leader in the Drone industry. Never in my wildest dreams did I personally think I would lead a tech company with a revolutionary aerospace platform, though I feel I positioned myself and the team strategically to increase the odds of success and making it happen.

What are some of the barriers you have had to overcome along the way? What inspired you to start your own Drone Business? What challenges did you have to overcome?

The barriers are endless in the startup phase whether that is financing, knowledge gaps, manpower and flat out mistakes in product development. We overcame these barriers by seeking out the 'Desert Rotor' advocates who believed in the company and supported us informally by reaching into their networks to help solve technical problems and offering solutions. The Desert Rotor team is fortunate to have deep networks throughout Arizona and the world. When we hit walls, we would find the appropriate people to help get us over it. Having confidence and being positive eases tension within the team and helps towards finding the right solution.

Let's talk business!   Tell us about your company; what should we know?

Look out for services in the future like remote piloting support to anywhere on the planet and breakthrough new features with the 12PCX HOTAS platform. We strive to offer the physical network infrastructure to collect and disseminate real-time data from Drones. Our systems allow companies to monitor and view the data coming off their Drones live and in real-time. Our goal is to offer high quality, high compatibility and cost-effective GCS platforms.

Any advice you can share for those seeking to get into the Drone business?   Perhaps your Top Do's and Don'ts

Do NOT discount ANYONE. Treat every level of professional with respect and importance. In a rather small unestablished industry many know each other and you never know who anyone will eventually become. First encounters are lasting. Too often "professionals" are abrupt, rude, condescending, disrespectful and flat out arrogant. Treat the college student who is doing research as if they were a large company CEO. It'll pay off. I can't tell you how many interactions I've had where most would think it's a waste of time and it ended up being a large client, supplier or referral down the road. Only build bridges.

The Drone industry is full of fresh ideas and many are pitching each other. Listen and truly seek ways how these ideas could fit with your business and theirs. Some ideas that seem outlandish can make more sense in the future.

Do network as much as possible. It is absolutely worth it to attend the large industry conferences to collect contacts and market research. There is a powerful connection made when you meet a person face-to-face, even if just for a few minutes. It goes a long way when communicating via strictly e-mails and phone calls to do business with people you've met. Looking back there are key events where if I hadn't gone to a meeting, conference or even hanging out with friends, that Desert Rotor wouldn't have happened. It is key to suck it up and get out there physically when possible.

Do your homework. If you are going to start a Drone business, you have to live and breathe your target market and target application. Drone pilots are expected to be experts in the respective field they are promoting, not just Drone piloting. For example, if you don't know anything about farming or can't offer crop consulting, agriculture might not be a good fit unless you are willing to study the field passionately. Too many Drone manufacturers and pilots just throw an aircraft or service at the wall and hope it sticks. You

HAVE to be an expert in that specific field to successfully integrate your products and services.

Marketing, please share any creative ideas that you have used for marketing your product.

Almost all our clients came to us through social media or word of mouth. Social media is an inexpensive way to get in front of thousands of people with just a few dollars. I recommend taking courses and/or studying Buyer Motivations, SWOT and various other marketing strategies that companies utilize. Case studies found in business publications can get your creative juices going towards your marketing campaign. There is a lot of psychology around marketing; it's best to learn as much as you can about it.

Desert Rotor has also found success with the little things when marketing. Custom company branded "swag" can go a long way at conferences. Not the basic pen, t-shirt type marketing - Be creative! At the Las Vegas conferences Desert Rotor got custom branded poker chips made with nicely branded microfiber cloths. This was unique and very memorable to our leads because no other company did that.

With the advantage of hind-sight, what would you do differently if anything?

In hind-sight I would have tried to build a larger team starting in 2016. We were tight financially as we were bootstrapping and I was investing a large percentage from my day job salary. Looking back, I could still have sought out more professionals who believed in the vision and were willing to do some sweat equity work. Sweat equity in our case would be efforts towards building the company that would be rewarded in partnership /ownership in Desert Rotor instead of initially taking a salary. The extra help would have gone a long way

Any shout-outs? Who else deserves credit?

The team, of course, deserves the most credit with Desert Rotor. Everyone has their part and all together it is a very powerful force. There is no way I could drive Desert Rotor alone, without the engineering team along with our operational crew. We do have a shout-out for the Sun Valley Fliers club. There are countless brilliant professionals there who we are fortunate to call best friends. Our best friends helped us in countless different capacities from the business end to highly technical challenges. It has also provided a friendly, awesome atmosphere when test-flying and pushing our GCS platform.

Bob Schmidt, President and Founder
UAV Propulsion Tech,
www.uavpropulsiontech.com

Bob Schmidt is the President and Founder of UAV Propulsion Tech. Bob has a Bachelor of Science in Mechanical Engineering (BSME) from Lawrence Technological University, a Master of Science in Administration (MSA) from Central MI University, and has over 30 years experience in development, sales and marketing of fuel/propulsion systems for powersports, automotive and military applications. Bob is always looking for new non-US companies with advanced UAV technology that are looking for a representative in the US.

Bob's company, UAV Propulsion Tech is a US based company located in Tampa, FL that markets advanced UAV technology from Germany, Austria, India, Canada, Sweden, United Kingdom, France and Estonia into the US Unmanned Aerial Vehicle market. These solutions include consumer off the shelf (COTs) and custom hardware solutions that are flying on several high-end global UAV platforms.

Briefly walk us through your story – how you started and how you got to where you are today

I am a mechanical engineer and started my career in the automotive fuel system business working for several key automotive suppliers (Walbro, now TI Automotive and VDO-now Continental AG). I started working on throttle body mass air flow sensors, later transitioned to the development of fuel pumps (even spent a short time as an expat working in France supporting the European automotive fuel pump market) and finished managing an engineering team developing new fuel delivery modules in Michigan. I left in 2000 and started working for Orbital Australia, heading up their US business development. Orbital has a unique direct injection system that was used on 2-stroke engines to reduce emissions and 4-stroke automotive engines to reduce fuel consumption. In 2003 we started working on a program with Mercury Marine to help them calibrate their OptiMax outboard (that used Orbital's DI system) to work on JP5 (jet fuel) for the US Navy. We learned that the air-assist DI system enabled spark ignition operation on jet fuel. We later applied the technology to Hirth aircraft engines to support the UAV market. In 2007, Orbital wanted to reduce their US marketing costs so I switched from employee to contractor. I became a representative of Orbital and also Hirth at this time. As I made contacts in the industry, I started adding more companies to my business, UAV Propulsion Tech, to provide their solutions to the US market. I was typically focused on smaller non-US companies that had a unique technology and were looking for someone to market their UAV hardware products into the US. I now offer over 50 products from 8 different countries. I also manage the LinkedIn group "UAV TECH".

What are some of the barriers you have had to overcome along the way?

The market can be cyclical and this is the reason I keep adding more solutions. I want to be the one stop shop for UAV hardware. Kind of like Bosch and other automotive suppliers are for the auto business. Other barriers are company budgets for new UAV development. Most are done on a shoestring until they get a customer interested which means they start with lower cost RC engines/servos instead of starting with a high end reliable solution developed for the market. Also, since most of the hardware I supply is built to order, timing can be a barrier to new business. I can lose business to an inferior competitive product just because it was available in a shorter time.

What inspired you to start our own Drone Business? What challenges did you have to overcome?

I was forced to start my own business when I was asked to become a contractor instead of an employee. This forced me into more of a sales mindset because if I didn't sell, I wasn't going to make any money or survive. I was lucky in getting some great sales with my efforts with Orbital, Hirth and Volz which allowed me to gain a reputation in this market and be able to offer other technology solutions. I hope to be able to offer fuel system hardware and engineering solutions Q2 of 2018.

**Let's talk business. Tell us about your company–
what should we know?**

I am the founder and president of UAV
Propulsion Tech, an unmanned aerial vehicle (UAV)
hardware solution provider of propulsion, servo,
autopilot, rescue/recovery parachutes, electric
turbofans, pneumatic launchers, capacitive liquid level
sensors, ultrasonic fuel flow sensors, engine sensors,
gyro-stabilized EO/IR gimbals, inertial navigation
systems, Galileo digital magnetic compass hardware
and remote operated submersible vehicle solutions.

**Any advice you can share for those seeking to get
into the Drone business? Perhaps your Top Do's
and Don'ts**

Don't mortgage your house. I was lucky and
my business didn't require any significant funding to
start/maintain. I don't need a brick/mortar facility, I
don't have to stock inventory of hardware and I am not
manufacturing anything. I would say do as much as
you can on a shoestring with your own money. Maybe
work for a larger company to gain some experience. I
don't provide drone services like so many individuals
and companies are going after at the moment, so
unfortunately, I cannot provide any advice for that
market.

Marketing, please share any creative ideas that you have used for marketing your product?

I am mainly targeting large aerospace/defense companies that may need my hardware so I use several ways to promote my business.

- First, I have a detailed LinkedIn page and am building lots of global connections on this platform. I also moderate the LinkedIn group UAV TECH to increase my exposure and credibility in this market.

- I have a Twitter account (@schmidtproducts) and follow other drone/UAV businesses and tweet almost daily on key UAV news and promotion of my business.

- Some of the companies I represent advertise in print (like Shephard's Unmanned or Unmanned Systems Technology magazine) and add my contact info. I advertise on UAS Vision's daily email (banner ad) and I have a listing on www.unmannedsystemstechnology.com.

- I promote my solutions via my Blog. I try to do a blog at least once a month on my website:

- I have a company listing on LinkedIN for UAV Propulsion Tech.

- I attend and exhibit at trade shows. Four of the companies I represent have exhibits that I support (Hirth, Volz, DST Control, MicroPilot). The largest UAV show in the world is AUVSI's XPonential.

- I exhibit at smaller trade shows like regional AUVSI (like Pathfinder in Huntsville) and SOFWERX.org here in Tampa, FL.

- I attend select global trade shows where my rep companies are exhibiting like: AUSA (USA). IDEX (AbuDhabi, UAE), DSEi (London, UK), Heli-Expo (USA), Interdrone (USA), SOFIC (USA), Commercial UAV Expo (USA)

With the advantage of hind-sight, what would you do differently if anything?

I should have added complimentary products earlier. I originally was focused more on the propulsion side (Hirth/Orbital) but as you add other products, you gain exposure to more customers and learn more about the complete system.

Any shout-outs? Who else deserves credit?

Chris Harris from NWUAV is a friend, customer and a competitor. In the UAV/Drone business you will find a close knit group of technical people that are always willing to help each other. Don't be afraid to ask questions.

CHAPTER NINE
Learn From Other Miners
Modeling Success

Our past experience in running our own company told us that focusing on what other companies have done to be successful or what we refer to as "Modeling Success" can be a valuable tool in starting a company. We started Argus Rising in 2015 and at that time there were no "First Responder" Drone Training Companies to model. However, at the core of our company is training so we selected several of the top training companies along with other successful companies that have redefined their business. The "Do *something, anything, differently*" companies in the US are plentiful and from those models, we architected Argus Rising. This is a great idea for anyone who's planning a business. Study successful corporate competencies, processes and cultures, and where it makes sense strive to emulate them. There's nothing wrong with emulating success.

Those who've read our previous book, Be A Wolf, know that we did this with Southwest Airlines when we were structuring our culture. We visited their corporate headquarters and got tons of ideas of how to generate employee interest in achieving a standard of excellence. Today Southwest Airlines is still ranked in the top ten of companies with people-focused cultures. They have been in business for over 50 years and people still love working for them. Knowing some of these people personally, it's not hard to see that they feel invested in the success of their company.

The former Southwest President and CEO Herb Kelleher helped found the company in the early seventies, and he successfully shepherded Southwest through airline deregulation, 9/11, economic recessions, and astronomical fuel prices. His philosophy for success was simple but incredibly effective: *Happy workers take care of customers.* Apparently he's right, because Southwest Airlines has repeatedly been named one of the best companies in America to work for by *Fortune* magazine, and they are one of the few profitable airlines still in the air. The much-beloved Kelleher, who left to outrageous cheering and applause (and not a few tears, including his own), doesn't hesitate in attributing Southwest's success entirely to its employees. He knows that Southwest's most important asset is its people.

Allow us to repeat that yet again. It doesn't matter if you have two employees or two thousand: YOUR MOST IMPORTANT ASSET IS YOUR PEOPLE.

Creating a people-focused environment means that you are invested in the success of your people; when they know there is support at the top, motivated employees will help make your company strong and will ensure that customers and clients report high satisfaction ratings. It also means that you must evaluate the strengths of your employees and guide them to achieve expertise in their field that can then be shared with the team. This doesn't mean that you give up decision-making; it means that you consider well-advised input that you trust. Your company needs a strong leader; your employee's career success and the success of your company go hand-in-hand.

Knowing the value of a 'people-first' culture, we repeated that when we built Argus Rising. We didn't do it the same way, but we got the same results We wanted our employee incentive program to publicly recognize and reward success. but to be truly unique. At start-up we viewed ourselves as Rogue Drone Entrepreneurs and wanted our incentive program to reflect that. Year One before we had made a penny, we opted to take the entire team to InterDrone in Las Vegas. From this base, employees have been able to determine their avenue of interest and to translate that into how their skills and interests can be incorporated into the company goals. We attended seminars in teams and sometimes individually, comparing notes and becoming more specific towards the end of the week in areas we felt we could use and build upon. Following that first conference, we collaborated weekly on core-knowledge and expansion of that knowledge.

Communications between you and your team is primary and key to developing a framework for who's doing what – particularly in a small business. Get your people pointed in the right direction, let everyone know what role various team members are fulfilling and set expectations. Maintaining a people-oriented culture must be maintained day in, day out, as you run the business. Your company culture should be evident in everything you do, from your style of leadership to how you make decisions to your hiring and firing practices.

One thing we did from the beginning was actively encourage an "open door" policy. The last thing we want is to be the stereotypical remote execs who dictate orders from behind closed doors. We've found that the Drone business is more "hands-on" than our previous business, mainly because the market is so open and opportunities are so abundant that you have to set your GPS and use First Person View and not Autopilot. You can definitely consider a detour; but if approved, you must communicate that change to the entire group with all roles adjusted to keep your company goals intact. We have FAA Drone Pilots License even though we rarely fly Drones these days. We built the business from the ground up, and somewhere along the way we have been a part of every project that the company has undertaken. We've made it our business to know our business inside-out.

Although our main source of communication within the company is emails and texts, we are also active on social media sites where we keep our clients and employees attuned to what's happening within the Argus Rising world, as well as current trends in Drones, particularly in relationship to the Law Enforcement / Fire Rescue interests. While social media is relatively new to us, we understand its importance; don't make the mistake of ignoring social media sites as a tool to keep your company in front of your audience. Social media is here to stay – be at the top of your game.

Here's the deal, plain and simple: *a people-focused culture is an investment in your business*. We think it's the best investment you'll ever make. We spend a lot of money on our company culture and we have fun, but we're not a party company and we've never thrown a single dollar away. We firmly believe that every penny we spend on company culture returns to us a hundredfold. Our first year, we took our employees to InterDrone in Vegas before we had made a penny. But we didn't hesitate a second. This trip was the Argus Rising way of saying "we are family" and we are jointly invested in our mutual success. On this we refuse to compromise, and we're so glad we don't, as the return on the investment is plain for all to see. Our company culture attracts good people, encourages loyalty, and as a result, increases productivity. Simply put, happy employees are not only productive, they are inspired to help make Argus Rising the best of the best.

Where do our *customers* fit in to all this talk of company culture and employee satisfaction? Well believe it or not, we've been discussing our customers all along! Herb Kelleher is right: happy workers take care of their customers. We'll go one step further and say that happy workers give *consistently superior* customer service. There's no question that workers who feel valued and who feel they are taking part in meaningful work are more productive, more loyal, and perform at the top of their game. Our company culture encourages exactly this kind of performance, and our team members rarely let us down.

In fact, overall instructor performance has achieved levels way beyond our expectations, and the benefits of the Argus Rising culture just keep on giving. Even as a small, fledgling company, Argus Rising was able to attract a lot of terrifically talented people. Then and now, top-notch people accept positions with us because they love the culture and our First Responder Focused Mission. Our people are actually the best advertisement we have. As our people spread the word that Argus is a great place to work, more and more talented people seek us out, then *they* spread the word, and so on. Our company culture attracts a fantastic pool of people, and we in turn enjoy an ever-increasing pool of talent.

What's more, once we'd established our company culture and saw how well it worked, it was largely self-perpetuating. You've probably heard before that success breeds success. That is certainly the case for Argus. Once employees understand the Argus way of doing things, they take an active part in maintaining our culture, and even branch off into creative ways of expressing it that we did not anticipate. The success the team has created together speaks to how well a people-focused culture works.

Here's just one story illustrating the kind of employee loyalty we've been privileged to receive. Way back when with our first company, the original Argus Connection, Allen was all by his lonesome in that tiny rented office, a man named Brian Twing worked down the hall. Brian would pass by the Argus office each day and, as we discovered later, think to himself, "Man, I hope that guy has better luck than the rest of them." Little did we know that we were the fourth business to start up in that cramped space, and Brian had watched each of our predecessor's fold. After ninety days, Brian noticed the empty office and shook his head, assuming we were yet another casualty in the often treacherous world of start-ups. Later that day he happened to run into Allen, who'd upgraded to a bigger office in the same building. Brian was so excited that Argus had merely moved and not gone out of business that he walked in and introduced himself. The two hit it off immediately, and Brian was soon as enthusiastic about Argus as we were. To make a long story short, two months later we hired Brian, and he worked for Argus for over eleven years. Twenty years later, Brian is now the Director of Research and Development for Argus Rising; his enthusiasm for Drones and our new Drone venture is inspiring for other company employees, as well as the two of us.

As a leader, recognize and reward individuals as well as team efforts that move your company closer to set goals. Don't be afraid to invest in your people by educating them, encouraging them and incenting them. The positive environment you cultivate will have outstanding results in the arena of client/customer loyalty and satisfaction.

Chapter Nine Notes:
Learn From Others Miners
Modeling Success

- There's nothing wrong with emulating success. This is a great idea for anyone who's planning a business. Study successful corporate competencies, processes and cultures; where it makes sense, strive to emulate them.
- Your most important asset is your people - Creating a people-focused environment means that you are invested in the success of your people; when they know there is support at the top, motivated employees will help make your company strong.
- Communications between you and your team is primary and key to developing a framework for productivity and loyalty, strive to build a company that attracts and retains talent, it is key to the long term success of any company.
- As a leader, recognize and reward individuals as well as team efforts that move your company closer to set goals. Don't be afraid to invest in your people by educating them, encouraging them and incenting them. The positive environment you cultivate will have outstanding results in the arena of client/customer loyalty and satisfaction.

CHAPTER TEN
Expansion
The Rules of Engagement

Once your start-up becomes stable, it's time to begin thinking about expansion. Even if you're only a few months into your entrepreneurial adventure, it's not too early to start planning for expansion with planning being the key word. Expansion or digging your mine deeper when you see additional opportunity is a good thing but keep the canary close by, there are actually plenty of businesses who went under when faced with unexpected or very rapid expansions.

In the business world, the size of your business requires a balancing act that must be monitored and managed closely. No growth means bankruptcy, while rapid business expansion can put you out of business as quickly as no business at all. It can be difficult to grasp how what may sound like the deal of the century can be your undoing especially if you're just starting out, but it's absolutely the case that a deal that promises an enormous payoff and precipitous expansion can cause a cave in. We are not saying "don't pursue the large gold vein" we are saying pursue it with caution.

Let's look at how this can happen. We will utilize a recent example. We were presented with an opportunity for a large global project by a company in London to see if we could provide these services:

- Turnkey industrial drone inspection of 100+ sites in 20 countries around the world but mostly in South America and the Middle East
- Consultation services on the production

- Implementation of corporate-wide UAV policies and procedures
- Training for 100+ internal employees who will operate UAVs for the company

This was an outstanding opportunity and while it would take us outside of our chosen niche of First Responder Training we could build separate dedicated full-time teams for the project and not impact our training schedule. A team would consist of 4 people that could travel extensively. We would likely field 3 teams or 12 full time people. A single team would consist of a Senior Training Lead, Photographic Lead, UAV Assistant and a Project Manager. We calculated it would cost $24,750 per site assuming we could schedule the sites back-to-back with no single site taking more than 6 days. Any site that required more than 6 days for any reason would incur an additional charge of $4,125 per day. Quickly do the math; this is a $2 Million plus opportunity.

Everything looked great and all systems were set for an immediate go. That is, until we loaded the cost and expected cash return of the deal into a spreadsheet. The results were dismal; this project would consume cash like no tomorrow in the form of payroll and travel. Lots of red flags were appearing and it could easily run through our cash reserves in just 6 weeks.

Why? We needed to hire additional people to get the job done and would not get paid until after each site was completed. It could easily take 8-12 weeks before payment would be received. So, let's look at a possible project ramp-up and payment schedule:

- We hire and train the pilot team for 3 weeks prior to the first field engagement
- We run 5 pilot sites to fine tune and document the processes for follow-on teams
- We would invoice $24,750 after each pilot site was completed
- Average team cost for 1 week $12,000 + Travel

We will be 4 weeks into expenses before we even get to send an invoice. Our experience says that the first invoice of any new project will take 90 days to get paid and although this timeframe will decrease over time, it will likely never be less than 6 weeks. So, we will be 11 weeks into the pilot project before we receive our first payment for $24,750.

At eleven weeks, our expenses would already be $170,000 [11 weeks X weekly payroll of $12,000 = $132,000 plus travel of $38,000 for a total of $170,000]. That's a dismal picture.

Why so long before the first check? Anytime you deal with large corporations there is internal bureaucracy associated with getting a new vendor set up, validating services have been completed, etc. etc. On average that takes 90 days and that is how you should plan. If you get paid sooner, celebrate! However, you should use a 90-day receivables window after sending your first invoice. It will keep you from getting caught short. In a large deal like this one, lingering unpaid expenses will sink the ship.

Bottom line? The start-up investment required for this deal was more than we could afford. The deal that looked like it was going to catapult our company into the big-time would actually sink us within months.

This left us with two options. We could walk away, or we could go back and negotiate. We wanted the business, so it was time to get creative!

We set up a meeting with decision makers and let them know that the amount of upfront cash involved to provide these services would require a deposit payment of $400,000 paid to an escrow account that we could draw on immediately after the verified completion of each site. We then addressed travel expenses. Since travel was a pass through we requested the use of their company travel agency and credit card for all travel. This would cut our first receivables down to just 4 weeks from the first engagement and eliminate the travel expense.

- Once again, let's do the math, 3 weeks training and 1 week on-site = 4 weeks
- 4 weeks to our first payment but then our next payment would be one week later

So, let's do the pre-payment expenses again:
- 4 weeks times $12,000 = $48,000.

That's a lot more reasonable than $170,000. So, do we have a green light? I'm afraid not, there's more work to do on this one. You will need to spreadsheet the *entire project* from start to finish, all cash outlay, accounts receivable, expected payments all the way to the end of the project. Depending on the size of the project this can be a massive undertaking but you can't afford surprises. Sadly, at the end of the day they refused to provide an escrow payment. Interestingly they did agree to the travel option but that was not enough to carry the day, we walked away from this deal and sometimes that's what you have to do to stay in business.

The Rules of Engagement - This experience taught us several fundamental principles on how to expand. We called them the "Rules of Engagement", and together they make up the key to a successful expansion. If you want to expand your business safely and successfully, you must follow the Rules of Engagement with every deal you make:

1. Make favorable payment terms a part of your negotiation
2. Make sure the deal meets your profit criteria
3. Reduce your out-of-pocket expenses whenever possible
4. Perform a worst-case analysis
5. If it's a large deal like above, perform a "cash flow analysis" for the entire deal

If you're worried that practicing the Rules of Engagement for every deal will slow down the deal and cost you business, you can lay that worry to rest. If you build the Rules of Engagement into your daily business processes and practice them for each deal, completing the process for most opportunities requires very little time. If there's anything that derails the process, it's usually one of two things: your old nemesis, your ego (you don't want to see anything negative), or a client requesting unreasonable deadlines. Let's say you run into a deal you really want. It's low profit but it's with a high-profile company with a name you can brag about. You really, really want entry into this account, and you believe you can make up for the low profit with high volume. The client needs an immediate decision and signed contract, so you push it forward without evaluating cash flow impact, knowing you can borrow money if you have to. You sign the contract in haste, and guess what? You've just walked into the perfect storm. A perfect storm occurs when three or more negative factors come together in one deal. For this deal the perfect storm is:

1. Low profit
2. A client pressuring you for an answer
3. Failure to follow the Rules of Engagement
4. An ego-based decision

If it's a large deal, not many young companies survive the perfect storm so what you want to do is avoid it before it happens. Low profit is never optimal, and you should always determine your profit margin, with a buffer included. As for the ego-based decision, we already know the outcome. Suffice it to say that it's in your best interest to slow down, do your homework, and turn your attention to what's best for the business, not yourself. Next, remember that a client pressing you for a quick answer is a form of negotiation. Recognize the tactic for what it is and respond accordingly. Even when things are moving at lightning speed and you really, really want a deal, keep a cool head and practice your Rules of Engagement. Succumbing to an ego-based decision or making a hasty move without adequate homework is worse than simply letting a deal go. If enforcing your Rules of Engagement costs you a deal, then it's most likely a deal you did not want.

The final message we want to leave you with is that a crisis should never be automatically translated into failure. So often, people fold when they face their first business crisis. Don't let this happen to you. You're going to be faced with crises large and small when you go into business for yourself—this is just part of running a business. Knowing this, work to ward off crises before they materialize, and when they do, work to minimize them as quickly as possible. If you make a habit of practicing the Rules of Engagement with every deal, you'll avoid a whole host of business-breaking mistakes. The Rules of Engagement are there to help you expand your business with a minimum of mistakes and a maximum of gain. They're there to help you survive *and* thrive.

Chapter Ten Notes:
Expansion - *The Rules of Engagement*

- Rapid business expansion can put you out of business as quickly as no business at all.
- The Rules of Engagement are the key to safe and successful business expansion. They can be modified to work with any business, and they should be practiced with each and every deal.
- If you build the Rules of Engagement into your daily business practices, they can be followed expeditiously. It's a good idea to document your Rules of Engagement and if you have a sales team have your sales team sign off on them. You can even enforce a penalty if a team member fails to follow the Rules.
- Don't ever let your ego or a client pressuring you to conclude a deal lure you into failing to follow the Rules of Engagement. If the Rules ever "cost" you a deal, count your blessings: it's probably not a deal you wanted anyway.
- Never allow crisis to equal failure. You will always face crises in business, especially when you're just starting out. Let the Rules of Engagement help you avoid costly mistakes as well as gain lucrative deals that can safely expand your business.

EPILOGUE

It's Time to Join Us in The Adventure!

Company culture, start-up funding, making a sale, managing cash flow, marketing, expansion, ...the list goes on. We've covered a great many of the nuts-and-bolts aspects of owning your own business, so now let us return to the source. We're talking about the source of why you wanted to go into business for yourself in the first place. We're talking about the unmistakable spirit of adventure that lights a fire in every entrepreneur's veins, the spirit within that inspires a desire to strike out on your own. If you've got the fire in your veins, you'll never truly be satisfied with anything less than making the leap into the exhilarating world of entrepreneurship. Make no mistake about it, launching and running your own business is some of the hardest work you'll ever do—we'll be the first to tell you that it will put your physical and mental capacities to their greatest test. But we'll also be the first to tell you that except for family, there are few things in life that are more rewarding than being an entrepreneur. We wouldn't trade one minute of this adventure for anything corporate America has to offer.

If you haven't already made the leap into owning your own business, now may be the time. There are undeniable benefits to launching a business associated with a technology boom such as Drones. Barriers to entry may be lower than ever before. Many Drone companies are offering deeply discounted products and services that can help you start and market your business. Whether launching a business is something you've always wanted to do, or whether the loss of a job, a retirement fund, or your benefits has you considering self-employment for the first time, acting sooner rather than later may be to your great advantage.

Don't be misled into thinking that only the big boys can get into the Drone game and remember, even these giants started small. We often think that large corporations dominate America, but the fact is that small businesses constitute "99.7% of all employer firms" in the United States. Small business is this country's very lifeblood, and small business survival is key to maintaining our economic health. In these days of globalization, rapid technological advances, and unprecedented opportunity for networking, the collective success of all the small successes in each Small Town, USA is truly felt around the world. When you become an entrepreneur, you may be going into business for yourself, but you're becoming a part of something much greater than yourself. You become part of a greater community of people who are deeply motivated by their passions, their visions, and a quest for creating success on their own terms.

Does this sound appealing? Does a life of adventure, creativity, challenge, resourcefulness, pride in your accomplishments, and financial independence sound like the kind of life you want? Then you've felt your inner spirit calling you and we urge you to answer.

Entrepreneurship is truly an adventure, one that you need to be prepared for. It's an adventure filled with success and failure, wins and losses, laughter and tears. It's an adventure of a lifetime, one you do not want to miss. We hope you'll **join us in this life of fulfillment and adventure.**

Our Vision is to change the world one entrepreneur at a time.

Our Mission is to help you find success the way you define it.

We want to do no less than help you find your Passion. Find your passion and you will find your wealth.

Join us in the adventure! Join us as an entrepreneur and enjoy a life of inspiration, challenge, and countless rewards!

About the Authors
Andrea and Allen Beach

Andrea and Allen Beach were the founders and owners of Argus Connection, Inc., a multi-million-dollar technology services and staffing company based in Dallas, Texas and Argus Rising, a First Responder Drone Training company based in Grapevine, Texas. Andrea has served as the company's CFO and Executive Vice President; Allen as the CEO and President. They are both native Texans and together have over sixty years of business experience, including thirty-eight years' combined experience starting and running their own business. The couple has a wonderful blended family of four married children and seven—and counting! — grandchildren. When not on the road they split their time between Dallas and their family home in Colorado.

Made in the USA
Columbia, SC
10 December 2019